Hush!
Hush!

Hush! Hush!

Jill Briscoe

ZONDERVAN
PUBLISHING HOUSE   OF THE ZONDERVAN CORPORATION
GRAND RAPIDS, MICHIGAN 49506

To those who pray for me—
some who are known and
deeply loved,
some who are unknown and
deeply appreciated

"Vespers" by A. A. Milne, from *When We Were Very Young*, is used by permission of E. P. Dutton & Co. and Methuen Children's Books Ltd.

Scripture references are from the King James Version.

Hush! Hush!

© 1978 by The Zondervan Corporation
Grand Rapids, Michigan

Library of Congress Cataloging in Publication Data

Briscoe, Jill
    Hush! Hush!
      Bibliography: p. 159
      1. Prayer.   I. Title.
BV210.2.B69   248'.3   77-27895
ISBN 0-310-21831-4

Printed in the United States of America

Contents

Foreword

"More things are wrought by prayer than this world dreams of," according to Tennyson. I agree. But like many other people, I have to admit that as great as prayer is, it does not come easily.

Jill and I were talking about this one day, and we both came to the conclusion that we needed to look into the whole matter of prayer to see if we could get it out of the realm of piety and into the world of reality. That we ought to pray more and better was beyond debate, but how to do so was a problem.

Prayer is a key concept in the Bible, so we had little difficulty deciding that we ought to get into the Bible to find out what it has to say on the subject.

Then something interesting happened. As we considered our own difficulties in this area, we thought of many of our friends in the church. They, like us, were having problems with prayer—not with the idea of prayer, the necessity of prayer, or the advantages of prayer, but with the matter of just getting around to doing it. In fact, we came to the conclusion that although the church in which we work was flourishing in many ways, it had some glaring weaknesses in the area of prayer. That's when Jill had one of her brainstorms. She decided to start an exploration of prayer—not on her own, but with a group of volunteers who would invest an hour a week studying the subject and doing what they studied.

The class was announced, and the response was instant and great. Sixty people signed up and over one hundred turned up—every kind of person imaginable.

There was a sprinkling of "old timers" who loved to work their way around the world each Wednesday night in the prayer meeting; but most of the volunteers were quick to admit that when it came to praying, they were in the amateur bracket. So with a happy sense of exploring the unknown, the course was set. After three months, many of the people said, "Let's do it again"—and so many others wanted to be involved that there was no alternative but to repeat the class. That was over a year ago, and we are still repeating. In fact, over five hundred have gone through the learning and practicing experience of prayer, and there are still people waiting in line!

While discussing the interest and the results one day, Jill wondered aloud whether other churches might be interested in the whole approach and, if so, whether she ought to put the story and the information in print. I encouraged her to do it, and here it is! By the way—you may feel I am a little biased about this because the author is my wife. You are right; I am biased. But I'm also her pastor, and I've seen what this approach has done for our church.

Stuart Briscoe

Introduction

Little Boy kneels at the foot of the bed,
Droops on the little hands little gold head.
Hush! Hush! Whisper who dares!
Christopher Robin is saying his prayers.

God bless Mummy. I know that's right.
Wasn't it fun in the bath tonight?
The cold's so cold, and the hot's so hot.
Oh! God bless Daddy—I quite forgot.

If I open my fingers a little bit more,
I can see Nanny's dressing-gown on the door.
It's a beautiful blue, but it hasn't a hood.
Oh! God bless Nanny and make her good.

Mine has a hood, and I lie in bed,
And pull the hood right over my head,
And I shut my eyes, and I curl up small,
And nobody knows that I'm there at all.

Oh! Thank you, God, for a lovely day.
And what was the other I had to say?
I said "Bless Daddy," so what can it be?
Oh! Now I remember. God bless Me.

Little Boy kneels at the foot of the bed,
Droops on the little hands little gold head.
Hush! Hush! Whisper who dares!
Christopher Robin is saying his prayers.

A. A. Milne

Our churches today are full of people like Christopher Robin, who go there to say their prayers. At the appropriate moment in the service the minister intones, "Hush, hush." It is time!

8

Christopher Robin begins: "God bless Mummy. I know that's right." Well, that's a good start. It's nice to know you're doing something right when you've heard all those sermons about fulfilling the conditions of prayer, and you wonder if you dare utter a peep for fear you'll say something wrong. It *must* be right to say "God bless Mummy," mustn't it? Yes, surely yes! But don't you think it's rather strange that Christopher Robin is still saying "God bless Mummy" twenty years later?

A. A. Milne's beautiful "Vespers" prayer is touching and poignant when a child is praying it. When you are very small, this is how it's meant to be: a sweet childlike faith, innocent "baby talk" communion, an expectation that the omniscient Father will understand needs and be interested in your world of mothers, fathers, dressing gowns, and bathtubs. But the Bible says when we become adults, we are to put away childish things (1 Cor. 13:11). Then why are there so many Christopher Robins in church? Now no one is denying that Mummy, Daddy, Nanny, and I all need God's blessings, but as we grow in Christ, we are intended, through prayer, to accomplish much more than these elementary blandishments on behalf of others.

When I first became a committed believer at the age of eighteen, I began to pray Christopher Robin prayers. "God bless Africa," I intoned fervently at one memorable prayer meeting. A mature Christian came up to me afterward and inquired, "Which part of that great continent is your concern? Which mission are you thoroughly informed about? Which particular tribal problem are you well-acquainted with? And what specific answers to your prayer requests have you received?" I realized "God bless Africa" was *not* going to be sufficient!

9

Next, Christopher Robin goes on to more important matters:

> God bless Mummy. I know that's right.
> Wasn't it fun in the bath tonight?

Isn't that something? So many of us who suffer from "Christopher Robinitis" find our thoughts wandering. And *what* they wander to, when they should be concentrating on the Almighty and issues of life and death, can be as irrelevant and irreverent as the water in the bathtub! We can waste God's listening time even further by telling Him a lot of information He already knows! For example, Christopher Robin's fascination with the bath water leads him to inform the All-Intelligent Being that "the cold's so cold, and the hot's so hot"!

Over and over again, those of us who have never "grown up" in our prayer life pass on facts to God that are almost idiotic in content. Is *this* what it's all about? Surely there is a way to corral wandering thoughts.

After another "God bless" prayer, Christopher Robin demonstrates an additional distraction syndrome.

> If I open my fingers a little bit more,
> I can see Nanny's dressing-gown on the door.
> It's a beautiful blue, but it hasn't a hood.

Now then! What do we have? A peeping Christopher Robin! Have you ever seen one of these in church? I have. I've been one myself. It's easy to peek, especially when the prayer time is long and boring.

As we open our fingers that "little bit more," we don't see Nanny's dressing gown on the door, but we *do* see Mrs. Smith's new dress or the fast-balding head of the organist, or we notice how funny Mr. Roberts looks when he prays! The only way we seem to be able to really concentrate is to be completely Christopher Robinish about it all and zero in on *me*. That *has* to captivate our attention!

> Mine [the dressing gown] has a hood, and I lie in bed,
> And pull the hood right over my head,
> And I shut my eyes, and I curl up small,
> And nobody knows that I'm there at all.

Notice that there is suddenly so *much* to talk to God about. I manage to tell Him what I'm wearing (as if He's blind), what size I am (twice as big as He sees me, I'm sure), how lonely I am (even though I've had a lovely day), and finally, knowing He can't possibly resist my final plea, I ask for a "God bless" on my little gold head!

> *Little boy kneels at the foot of the bed,*
> *Droops on the little hands little gold head.*
> *Hush! Hush! Whisper who dares!*
> *Christopher Robin is saying his prayers.*

Herein lies the root of the problem. Christopher Robin is "saying" his prayers. He has not yet learned to "pray" his prayers. Have I? Have you? Christopher Robin, this book is for both of us, and may we be forgiven a little boy's prayer as we begin our study together.

> Oh! *Thank you, God, for a lovely day.*
> And what was the other I had to say?
> I said "Bless Daddy," so what can it be?
> Oh! Now I remember. *God bless Me.*

Suggestions for Leaders

1. For a large class, there should be one experienced leader.*
2. Materials needed for each participant: a Bible, a notebook, a pen or pencil, and a copy of this book.
3. Divide the class into groups each time you meet. Let each group choose its own discussion leader or appoint them yourself.
4. Define clearly what you want the groups to do and circulate from group to group to ensure that the instructions have been understood and to answer any questions that might be raised.
5. Adapt the assignments as needed. Be flexible and innovative. Use your initiative and imagination.
6. Watch for "take-over artists." Change the discussion leader or sit in with such a group and help.
7. Remind the groups to keep to the point of discussion. It helps to bring the groups together periodically to report what they are learning.
8. Have a box for questions. Invite your pastor to visit the class and answer questions—or do it yourself!
9. Pray for the class. Be prepared.
10. Have fun!

*You do not need a large class or group to use this book. You may use it as an individual or in families and small groups. Don't be afraid to try.

A Personal Assessment

When we used this material in our church, we began each new session of the prayer workshop with an opening exercise: either a questionnaire, a letter to God, or just open discussion in the group as to their needs where prayer was concerned. The questionnaire was answered by five hundred people over the year and a half that I taught the course.

If you are leading a class, write the questions on the board and tell the participants to answer them in their notebooks. Then discuss the answers. (If you are leading a class, be sure to read page 12 for Suggestions for Leaders.)

Questions on Prayer

Here is a composite look at forty persons surveyed. These answers were typical of the whole five hundred.

1. *What is the purpose of prayer?*
    Most of the participants indicated that the purpose of prayer is communication with God. It was sometimes emphasized that this communication is based on a personal relationship with Him.
2. *Have you ever spent one hour in prayer?*
    Ten out of forty had spent an hour in prayer.
3. *Is it an effort to keep praying for more than ten minutes?*
    For twenty-seven out of forty it was sometimes or always an effort to pray for more than ten minutes.
4. *Do you like to pray, or is it a bore?*
    Thirty out of forty usually liked to pray. It depended

greatly on what they were praying about. (This seemed a strange affirmative when they had previously admitted that it was an effort to keep going for more than ten minutes!)

5. *What do your prayers consist of?*
Most prayers included praise or thanksgiving, intercession, requests, and repentance, to a greater or lesser degree. One person told us she sang. When asked what song, she replied in a beautiful soprano, "Help, help!"

6. *When do you do your praying?*
There was quite a variance in the times people prayed: anytime, night, morning and night, morning and throughout the day, and before retiring. "Whenever I find time" was a typical statement.

7. *What part do feelings play in your prayer life?*
For twenty-five out of forty, feelings played a major part. "When I don't feel a certain way, I don't pray," said one, summing up the majority's experience.

8. *Have you ever had any specific prayers answered?*
Thirty-six out of forty said that they had had specific prayers answered. Some were a little more vague: "Never really asked for anything specific" and "Yes, I think."

9. *Are there conditions of prayer?*
Two out of forty persons said there were no conditions of prayer, and four didn't know. When we asked them to name as many as they knew, there were many different answers: come humbly, in God's will, in Christ's name, must be a Christian, in the Spirit, talk but listen also, no known sin, set time limits, feel closer on knees, etc. Some other answers were: "I thought it was just a means of communication and could include or omit whatever you wanted."

"You shouldn't think God will answer with a direct yes or no."

"Time limits—I set dates as to when prayers have to be answered."

10. *What has been your experience of prayer corporately and alone?*

    a) *Alone.* The positive response outweighed the negative, but there were still fifteen out of forty who found prayer alone difficult in varying ways. "I feel it is a one-way street without a relationship or interaction taking place."

    b) *Praying with others.* The majority of responses were negative—many felt uneasy or found their minds wandering. They felt something was missing. There were some who enjoyed group prayers, but only twelve out of forty. "Most of the time it seems we are just saying the same old thing with little results." "I have trouble thinking of something to say. I pray almost by rote."

One of the most interesting answers I found was a note on the bottom of one of the questionnaires: "Having tried to answer these questions, I now see—Dear Lord, *how much I need this class!*"

Letters to God

Throughout the class, we collected the prayers of other people and also our own "homemade" ones. These were placed in a file for use in our classes. Sometimes a shy pray-er could be helped by reading his or her own prayer or someone else's. The written prayers were simply left on a table, where anyone could collect one as he entered the room.

A few of these "homemade" prayers are scattered throughout this book. They have been written from the heart by a cross section of people of all ages.

Here are some prayers from the first class, writing from their hearts their reasons for being there.

> *Dear God, Here I am hoping to get to know You more personally. . . .*

> *Father, I want to know what part I play in the answering of prayer. I've seen many prayers answered, positively and nega-tively, but I guess it's the waiting ones— how do I know if the delay is to teach me patience, or because my attitude hasn't changed, or because I haven't heard some-thing I should have? I often get confused, especially when others have my situation all figured out for me and feel I should do a certain something.*

Dear God, I am in this class because so many times I don't know what to say to You. . . .

Dear God, I'm taking this class because I feel my spiritual growth is being hindered by my prayer life. I know prayer is not mystical, but practical and realistic.

I am in this class . . . expecting to learn how to develop a consistent prayer life that extends beyond Christian clichés and is firmly rooted in the Spirit.

I've joined this class, Lord, to feel more comfortable about praying with other Christians. . . .

Father, I don't always understand how my prayers can help others. . . .

Dear God, I am here in this class with my wife because we want to live a life of prayer. We want to be more in tune with You so we can have a full and rich life together.

Heavenly Father, I feel that I often pray, not out of love or real concern, but out of a sense of duty. How often should I pray?

How long? I feel strangely guilty praying for people I hardly know, even though I know I should.

Take time—about ten minutes—to write out your reasons for participating in this study. Write them in the form of a prayer.

1

Where Do I Start?

Dear God,

It's really amazing that whenever I read Your letters in Your Word, it seems You could have just written them yesterday. I feel very close to You. You've had a big influence on the last month of my life, and I'm really looking forward to talking to You about it.

Love,
Your son

1

Where Do I Start?

Prayer is conversation with God. He speaks to us through His Word; we speak to Him through our words.

God listens to man's side of the conversation. He hears people who don't belong to Him. I know this because He heard my prayer when I didn't belong to Him, before I was a Christian. I became a believer by praying a simple prayer asking God to accept me and come into my life. Because I know God heard my prayer, I can encourage others who don't know Him to pray. People like Cornelius. People who have been praying to God all their lives and yet have never personally met the One to whom they pray. Because of what happened to Cornelius, we need to tell others that God will hear their prayers.

Turn in your Bible to Acts 10:1-4, and read it to yourself. Write down the answers to the following questions in your notebook; and then, if you are working in a group, discuss the information you have gathered.

1. *What do you learn about Cornelius' prayer life from verse 2?*
2. *What do you think God thought about this uncircumcised Roman soldier's prayers? (vv. 4,31)*
3. *How did God go about answering those petitions? What does this teach you about God's attitude toward a "real" seeker's prayer, whoever is praying it? (vv. 3,9-19,34-35,44-48)*

Maybe you have always "said your prayers," but like Cornelius have never been personally presented with an available relationship with the One at whom you have aimed those petitions! "Heaven on earth" begins to happen in your life when you are personally introduced to the Lord God who wants to walk and talk with you—in fact, live within you, by the Holy Spirit. Would you like to accept Him just as Cornelius did? Then let me help you in case you do not know what to say.

As a student at Homerton College, Cambridge, I wanted to accept Jesus Christ and His Holy Spirit into my life. I knew I was a sinner and needed forgiveness. A girl asked me if I would like to begin this relationship with Deity, and I told her I wanted to very much! But I didn't know how to start my side of the conversation. I didn't know what to say. I was feeling clumsy, awkward, and even a little bit stupid, so my friend offered to share a prayer that I could make my own. Here it is. You may use it, too.

If you are working on your own, take a few quiet moments now to pray the prayer—or to remember with praise the day you prayed something like it for yourself. If you are working in a group, allow a mo-

> *ment of silence to do this now. The leader can read
> the prayer aloud for the group if he or she wishes.
> Here is the prayer:*
>
> *"Dear God, I know Jesus lived a sinless life and
> died on the cross that my sins may be forgiven. I
> know I need to thank Him and ask Him to person-
> ally forgive me and accept me, even as I now accept
> His Holy Spirit into my life. Come into my heart,
> Lord, and begin to talk to me from within. Then,
> Lord, teach me to pray. Amen."*

I'm sure Cornelius' prayers became quite different after
his relationship with God was established that day. He
began to learn, as we begin to learn, that any relationship
without communication between the participants starves
to death. What greater misery can be imagined than mar-
riage partners who never speak to each other, children and
parents who avoid conversation, or people who are supposed to be friends sitting in silence, wondering what on
earth to talk about. Relationship depends largely on verbal
communication; and in man's relationship with God,
prayer is the verbal communication.

John the Baptist was one of God's greatest VIPs. Jesus
said so: "Of man born of woman—there is no greater!"

What were the characteristics of one of God's VIPs?
There were many: courage, humility, a certainty about
what he was supposed to be achieving; but one of the most
important characteristics was that of a "desert" life style.
We read in Luke 1:80, "[John] was in the deserts till the day
of his showing unto Israel."

There are other examples of the desert life style in the
pages of Scripture. And there are also illustrations of those
without it! There is Martha in Luke 10—irritated with her
sister, with her Lord, and, I am sure, with herself for being

irritated! She was always too busy to go to the "desert" and spend time with God.

Saul, having met Jesus on the Damascus road, became an absolute menace to the church. True, he was busy preaching and teaching, but observe the reaction to his ministry. He reminds me of a hot potato straight out of the fire! No one wanted to hold onto him for long. He was thrown from one lot of unbelieving believers to the next. They didn't dare believe he was for real. He took off on one of the speediest and most disastrous evangelistic campaigns on record. From Damascus to Jerusalem to Antioch and finally, to the churches' great relief, into the deserts of Arabia. Then and only then had the churches "rest" (Acts 9:31)!

Is there a Saul or two in your church? Oh, they may have a dramatic testimony, a glory story, and be loaded with talent and spiritual gifts, but the church is constantly in turmoil because of them. The answer is quite simple—they need a desert life style. When Saul came out of the Arabian wilderness years later, he came back to the same church with the Book of Romans in his heart and a new attitude. Then, and only then, he brought an edifying word instead of a divisive one. Then he began church planting instead of church leveling; and, incidentally, he was given a new name—he became the apostle Paul!

The Lord goes to extraordinary pains to get us alone. He will move heaven and earth to provide us a desert. He will ask us, beckon us, cajole us, command us, persuade us, or chase us there. He may even use the "desert" of a hospital bed where there is only one way to look—up! I don't know what it will take for you, but I do know that our greatest transactions take place *alone,* and you can't be a VIP without that desert life style.

24

Why not stop right now and pray this prayer for yourself: "God, I want to be one of Your VIPs. I know it will take a desert life style. That means discipline. But before I can begin to discipline myself, I have to want to be a VIP. I do want to be a VIP, God, and I know You desire that for me far more than I desire it for myself! So as You do Your part, help me to do mine. Amen."

But what, you may ask, do I do when I get to the desert? You *talk!* Now, a conversation with anyone is going to take time. Conversations are not usually dependent on age, clever words or lack of them, or even similar cultural backgrounds. Any two people can communicate if both are willing to do so. But it does take a decision to spend time together. The more time given to that, the better the relationship can become; and the better the relationship can become, the better communication should be!

No one has any more time than *you* have. It is the discipline and stewardship of your time that is important. The management of time is the management of self; therefore, if you manage time with God, He will begin to manage you.

J. B. Phillips says in Colossians 4:5, "Make the best possible use of your time." Psalm 31:15 says, "My times are in thy hands." This doesn't happen automatically. You have to put your time *into* those hands. It's not a question of whenever you can squeeze some time with God into your weekly schedule. It is a question of giving your weekly schedule to Him and letting *Him* squeeze other things out so that you two can begin to meet together.

The great example we have before us is the example of our Lord Jesus Christ. To begin with, He stepped from the dimension of eternity into time, that He might achieve *in* time eternal accomplishments. That is what time is for—to achieve those things for which the minutes, days, and hours are lent to us. At the age of twelve, Jesus said, "I must be about my Father's business." So must we, and there is no way we can do that unless time is spent asking the Father which part of His business we must see to each day.

Priorities determine your daily, weekly, and monthly schedule. Make a list of five of your responsibilities for today and five of the things you plan to do for yourself. Mark them honestly in order of priority, one to ten. There are 24 hours in a day; 168 hours in a week. If there are 56 hours to sleep, that leaves 112 waking hours. Distribute honestly the portion of time you give to the following per week: husband/wife or parents, children or family, work, leisure, personal time with God, God's service.

If you are working on your own, stop right now and ask yourself, Is God getting a good deal? Pray about that now.

If you are working in a group, discuss your conclusions for a few moments.

There are a number of examples in the Old Testament of busy men who made their time with God the number-one priority in their lives. The example of Daniel is perhaps the best pattern for us.

Turn to Daniel 6:4-15. Read it through; then answer the following questions:
  1. *Describe Daniel's prayer life. (v. 10)*
  2. *How do you know Daniel's prayer life was important to him?*
  3. *Is my time with God that important?*

I would honestly have to say that my "quiet time" is not worth a den of lions! Is yours? I would like mine to be!

Perhaps some of you have decided you have such irregular life styles that it is impossible to make a regular habit or discipline of a "desert" rendezvous with God. There is always the unexpected, the emergency, the interruption. But according to Daniel it is in the unexpected situation that you *react to certain habits formed in secret!*

I am sure Nehemiah had a "Daniel" habit, and it was this daily practice of being in touch with God that enabled him to link up with the wisdom he sought in a very dangerous situation.

Turn to Nehemiah 2:1-6, read it; then answer these questions:
1. What national problem did Nehemiah become aware of?
2. What was his first response?
3. Why did he have to answer immediately?
4. How would you describe this sort of praying?

Now it is time to talk to God about these things we have been learning. Spend five minutes either in quiet personal prayer or in conversational prayer around the group. Pray about what God has taught you from the lives of Daniel and Nehemiah.

In conclusion, we can say we need to be like Daniel and Nehemiah every day. We need to be constantly referring to God throughout our daily experiences. Our attitude of dependence will stem from our habit of daily devotions. Take your calendar each Monday morning and block off ten minutes every day of the week. As your schedule differs, so will the time you put aside for Him. So make an appointment on your calendar and then keep it! Be as conscientious about that as you are about your club or tennis dates! Start now and become a Daniel.

Then practice talking to God on an informal basis this week. Chat with Him. Just talk in your mind all day long about everything. He is "within" you, so you two can be having a great conversation. Use emergency prayers when needed. They are simple to learn. Here is one I use all the time: "Help!" Try it; He will help you, for He is your Counselor and Friend and is within you to help all that needs helping (and if you are like me, that means He's going to be very busy!).

Look up these two verses and write them out in your notebook:
1. *1 Thessalonians 5:17*
2. *Matthew 6:6 RSV*
Pray about them now.

2

A Vision of God

Dear God,

Thank You for the comfort of knowing that "Your will will not lead us where Your grace cannot keep us." If there's something You want us to do, You do it with us. And help us to remember that if You have asked us to do it, it's because You want us to do it.

Dear God,

I know I've told You many times before, but I had to write this one for the record. Thanks, Lord, for making my life complete. I can only express myself in the way I live, and even that is not enough. I can't wait to get to heaven to be able to listen to You speak to me verbally.

Love through eternity,
Stu

2

A Vision of God

"Where there is no vision, the people perish."
— *Proverbs 29:18*

In my husband's book *Getting Into God,* he gives a simple pattern for prayer: *P* for praise, *R* for repentance, *A* for asking for others, and *Y* for asking for yourself. He says praise is where we should start. Most of us reverse the whole procedure and "YARP" instead! If you check on your prayer time, this is probably the case. To praise, or worship, means to ascribe value or worth to an object—in other words, "worthship." For a person to be able to praise his God means he must believe the object of his faith is worthy of his praise. Therefore, it follows that the more he knows about the object, the more praise he will want to express!

The whole duty of man is to glorify God. Psalm 50:23

says, "Whoso offereth praise glorifies . . . God." A description of *how* a man can praise God is given in the Scriptures.

Work together in a group or in a notebook on your own.
1. Soul praise can take place without words; it is an attitude of the mind. Look up the following verses and read them aloud in the group or to yourself.
   a. Psalm 4:7
   b. Psalm 103:1
   c. Isaiah 29:13
2. Social praise. The Spirit of praise is a social spirit. The man who praises God desires to do so publicly. Look up the following and read:
   a. Psalm 34:3
   b. Psalm 40:10
3. Song praise. The spirit of praise is the spirit of song. In the Old Testament we find lyrical and musical forms of praise as in the Book of Psalms. In the New Testament and today as well psalms, hymns, and spiritual songs are used in praise. Look up Ephesians 5:18-20.

If we would learn to pray, we must first learn to praise. And if we would learn to praise, we must first have a true vision and some understanding of the true God. Although God is invisible, He chose to reveal Himself in many ways, one of which was to show a small glimpse of His glory through mystical visions. The result was a spontaneous and sincere acknowledgment of His worth by those most honored people who received such revelations, and a corresponding sense of their own unworthiness. We can share in these mystical visions as we read those particular passages of Scripture in our prayer time and meditate on what it was that these men saw. Think about the verbal pictures they drew for us and look for any aspect of what they saw that has significance. For example, Isaiah 6:1 says, "In the year that king Uzziah died I saw also the Lord sitting upon a throne, high and lifted up, and his train filled the temple." This reminds us of the position of the Lord—high above all.

---

1. Read one of the following passages to yourself:
   a. Isaiah 6:1-8
   b. Ezekiel 1:24-28
   c. Daniel 7:9-10
   d. Revelation 1:10-16
2. Silent contemplation and praise.
   A vision of God brings forth praise. What else does a vision of God do to a person? To find this out, we will see what reaction these men had to their visions.
3. Look up the following verses and write out your answers; then share what you find with your group.
   a. Isaiah 6:5
   b. Ezekiel 1:28
   c. Daniel 8:18
   d. Revelation 1:17

Conclusion: A vision of God results in a vision of ourselves. It cuts us down to size and gives us true perspective.

Another way we can have a vision of God is by studying the Scriptures. We can begin to understand His worth through a realization of His character in the revelation of the Old Testament, and further as we watch Him in action through the gospel narratives. A biblically illiterate person will not easily bring forth praise.

It is through the Bible, then, that we can come to know how much we have to praise God for, not only His *being*, but His *doing*. We can cultivate praise by fixing our hearts on God (Ps. 57:7) and by meditating on His ways and works. It is, however, through quiet contemplation of His work on the cross for us that praise can best be born. We don't need a mystic vision. We can "see" God through the biblical revelation of His attributes.

Look up as many of these verses as possible. Find and write down each attribute of God that is mentioned:
1. Who He is
    - a. Genesis 17:1
    - b. Genesis 21:33
    - c. Exodus 34:6
    - d. Joshua 3:10
    - e. John 17:25
    - f. Romans 15:5
    - g. Romans 15:13
    - h. Romans 15:33
    - i. 1 Corinthians 1:9
    - j. 2 Corinthians 1:3
    - k. 1 John 4:8

Share your findings with the group.

Spend a few moments in the group or alone praising God for His character or who He is. (The leader may begin one-sentence prayers with: "O Lord, we want to praise You for who You are." One word or one sentence may follow. For example, "Thank You for Your holiness, Lord," etc.)
2. What He has made
    We can see God in His handiwork. Look up and read Psalm 19:1-6. Spend time this week in the Book of Psalms contemplating what God has made.
    - a. His power manifest. Read Psalm 77 together or in private. The psalmist is in trouble. What

---

34

> helps him at this time? Write a summary of this
> psalm.
> b. His Providence shown. Read Job 38—41 on
> your own or in pairs.
> 3. What He has done
>   We can see God in His loving action toward us in
> redemption. Choose a passage to read and meditate
> on.
>
> | | | | |
> |---|---|---|---|
> | a. | Psalm 22:1-23 | e. | Matthew 27:33-44 |
> | b. | Isaiah 50:4-8 | f. | Matthew 27:45-50 |
> | c. | Matthew 26:36-42 | g. | John 18:19-24 |
> | d. | Matthew 27:27-32 | h. | John 19:1-7 |
> | | i. Philippians 2:5-8 | | |
>
> *Praise God for what He has done for you from each
> passage. If working in a group, each choose a different
> aspect to praise Him for and spend a few moments in
> prayer together.*

Conclusion: When it is hard to praise God for what He
allows to happen in our lives, we can praise Him for who
He is, what He has made, and what He has done.

Prayer, then, must commence with praise. However,
some people today tend to take the expression of praise to
an extreme. I personally react negatively toward bright
shiny Christians telling me they have learned to praise
God for anything from leukemia to a divorce! How can we
praise God for those things He weeps over? On earth Jesus
wept at death, was angry about the hardness of people's
hearts which caused divorce, and condemned those who
exploited the weak. Perhaps what these modern "prais-
ers" are really trying to say is that it is possible to find God
in every dark situation. To see Him high and lifted up and
to praise Him for who He is and for what we can learn of

Him in the dark circumstances is not to praise Him for the darkness itself!

A friend who has been a missionary in France for a long time told me of an extremely difficult set of circumstances that led her to inquire of a fellow worker, "How can you be so serene when everything has collapsed around you?" "Well," the fellow missionary replied, "when I can't praise God for what He allows, I can always praise Him for who He is 'in' what He has allowed." That helps. Try it!

Another good reason for praising God is that praise keeps the credit where it is due. Remember, he who offers praise glorifies God. I'll never forget doing a Bible study on the crowns that will be the rewards in heaven for faithful Christians. What an exciting discovery it was for me to see the good things awaiting us in eternity—rewards for such things as hospitality, martyrdom, evangelistic effort, and even a reward for those who "look for His coming." That last one should be easy to win!

I began to have a vision of God patting my head as He piled on the crowns, the weight of which surely would give me an eternal headache! There I would be, sitting smugly in heaven with all that gold giving me justified glory! Well, that didn't sound quite right, so I began to think again. Not one reward would I ever receive that had been obtained without His enabling, His gifts, or His grace. Not one victory won that He had not fought for me, not one soul brought to life without the regenerating operation of the Holy Spirit. Not one. Not one!

As I read Revelation 5, I saw the twelve elders, representing (some believe) the church. Sitting around that glorious Being on the throne, they appeared to be well and truly crowned. What then? Seeing the Lord high and lifted up and His train filling the temple brought the only possible response. Rising, they fell on their faces and cast their crowns at His feet where they truly belonged.

I decided that day I would not wait till I sat in glory. If men ever gave me a crown, I would cast it at His feet. It would be His anyway.

One day I was asked to address a meeting for the Fellowship of Christian Athletes. Sportsmen and women from all over the country would be there, together with their coaches, wives, husbands, and family members. They would gather together for one glorious weekend of fellowship. Since in those days I was struggling with my ability to speak to mixed groups, I found I desperately wanted a crown of approval from those men. I knew how hard it was for some of them to be spoken to by a "mere woman." I wanted so badly to do a good job! Then I read Revelation 5 again on my knees.

At the end of my talk, I told the group about my struggles. I shared with them that I had cast that particular crown at His feet *before* I came to the podium. It didn't matter any more. All that mattered was the coal from the altar, spoken of in Isaiah 6. He had touched my lips and demanded my obedience to "go for Him." Why, then, should I look for a crown? *His* is the command, *His* the enabling, *His* the cleansing, *His* the message, and if any blessing, *His* the praise. Men could give what they would—or wouldn't. All that mattered was that the *Lord* be high and lifted up.

Praise enables us to keep ourselves in true perspective and to give credit where it is due. Praise ye the Lord! And hallelujah!

3

An Acrostic on Praise

Dear God,

You have made me who and what I am. You chose my parents and my environment. You led in my paths of learning for Your glory. Now You have called me to have a relationship with You, to obey You, to hear You, to see You, and to learn of and respond to You. Hear now the pleadings of my heart. I have only come half way. I walk with eyes closed and fingers in ears. Soften my heart to Your call, forgive my attitude to my brother, and lead me in right paths for Your glory and praise.

In Christ's name,
Chuck

3

An Acrostic on Praise

P stands for Prepare

> Look up Matthew 6:6 and write it out. Take a few moments to discuss or write about the "place" of prayer in your house. Discuss or list the problems involved in finding a place!

When I was a young missionary mother, we lived in a small house. It was the sort of place that made you feel as if you had at least fifty children, when you knew for a fact you had only three! We shared our home with various people whom God sent into our lives, and we enjoyed what could best be described as "close" fellowship. In fact, if a definition of fellowship is "two fellows in a ship," we felt as though there were one hundred fellows all in the same vessel!

41

Hush! Hush!

At that time all of our children were under school age, and we were enjoying a typical English winter, which was good for ducks but a bit damp for human beings. Thus we were all confined indoors for days on end. I remember reading Matthew 6:6 and feeling desperate: "But thou, when thou prayest, enter into thy closet, and when thou hast shut thy door, pray to thy Father who is in secret; and thy Father who seeth in secret shall reward thee openly!" The only places in our house that were secret *were* the closets, but they were so full of clothing, children's toys, and junk that it required fortitude just to open one of them. There had to be a place somewhere, I remember thinking. Just a space I could be "apart," untouchable by sticky fingers or a crawling baby. Away from the teen-age problems of our lodgers—just for a *few* minutes!

Then my eye lighted on the children's playpen. It was ideal. So I got *in* and put them *out!* Of course the little imps started rattling the bars furiously to get at me. (As far as I can remember, that's the only time they tried to get *in* instead of escaping!) But I was safe. It was a little oasis of space. Just a few mind-saving moments so that I could share some "secrets" with the Father and receive some encouragement from Him. Then I was ready for the battle again as I clambered ungracefully, but renewed, out of my open-air closet!

I don't care how small your house is, or how noisy the kids, there will be a place. Find it! Name it! Tell Jesus you'll see Him there! Prepare—plan a place and time with Him.

R stands for Remember

"Be still and know that I am God." The Bible says praise will spring to our lips when we remember. This requires

an exercise of the will to shut out Christopher Robin in-
anities and mundanities and fix our minds on Him.

Read Psalm 77, then fill in the answers in your
notebook. If you are in a group work in pairs.
1. Make a list of Asaph's problems and distresses
   (vv. 2-4).
2. In verses 5-9 doubts crowd in. God has been
   good to Asaph in the past. But now he fears —
   what (vv. 7-8)?
3. In verse 10a, Asaph sums up his distress and
   doubt with a statement: "This is my infirmity."
   Then comes the glorious "but." Write in your
   notebook the statement in verse 10 beginning
   with the word but. Then make a list of the things
   he remembers (vv. 11-19).
In verse 20 Asaph comes trotting up to his Shepherd again. He remembered enough to realize that he,
the lamb, was ever led, though the way be dark, by the
Good Shepherd.

Conclusion: If praise is an antidote for depression,
which I believe it is, then how does it work in practice? It
works in part as we deliberately *remember* our blessings
and name them one by one!

Stop now in the group, or on your own, and in
quietness remember one by one some characteristics of your heavenly Father, or some manifestly
loving action of His toward you. Think about a
prayer He has answered or gift He has given you. This
positive activity will surely help to lift your heart in
praise.

43

Hush! Hush!

A stands for Adore.

The root meaning of *adore* comes from the Latin *orare*, "to speak to." Adoration then involves the idea of the articulation of a worshiper, an ardent admirer, or a lover. Another sense of adore is to salute someone with the highest respect. Now it is time to articulate with our mouths and salute our God!

> *Start in the group, or aloud if you are alone, using praise-sentences that address God in adoration:*
> *e.g., "I worship Thee, O High and Holy One,"*
> *or, "I approach Thee in awe, O Majesty on high,"*
> *or, "I salute Thee in wonder, O Deity," etc.*

I believe there is a time for talking one-to-one to God as a Friend, but just try to remember it is always *One-to-one*. We can get too "chummy" with Deity, and we do well to adore Him, to venerate and esteem Him, remembering His holiness and unapproachability, His otherness, His majesty and Godhead. Now is the time to do this. Incidentally, I never feel quite right if I adore Him while seated. Somehow, it helps to stand or kneel. Occasionally it does no harm to be prostrate on one's face! It is not necessary, but it somehow serves to remind us of who God is and the relationship that exists between us.

Once we were working on a teen-age musical drama, and the cast was becoming sloppy and erratic in performance, complaining in their attitudes, and had begun to lose the effectiveness of their ministry. Gathering them together, I challenged them to a new commitment to their Lord. "Let's pray about it together," I concluded. They readily acquiesced. "Let's pray on our knees," I suggested. I found out not one of these church-oriented kids had ever done that.

An Acrostic on Praise

"Does physical position make any difference?" one asked.

"Not to God," I replied. "He's so anxious to hear a squeak out of some of us that He won't care if you're upside down doing the splits in a tree! But I find it does help to remember who's needing Who!" We knelt and prayed.

Suddenly I heard a muffled sound. I looked up. One of the kids had prostrated himself flat on his face before his God. He began to pray thus, "O God, I cannot get lower before You than this." It was a broken prayer from a broken boy. It was a fervent request for restoration. The play was different after that! No wonder, for the Bible says, "The effectual *fervent* prayer of a righteous man availeth much" ("fervent" means "stretched out").

> *So let us kneel and pray. Let us articulate our adoration. Let us remember to whom we dare to speak. Let us salute Him now by spending a few moments in silent praise.*

I stands for Imagination

Imagination is like useless Christmas presents—those things people give you which you haven't a clue what to do with, like a fabulous butterfly in a glass case. You know it's valuable, but you haven't any idea how it could fit into your decor. You have to keep it because it's too good to just give away or put in a cupboard—which you'd love to do if the people who gave it to you didn't come over so often! You feel guilty about it all and end up wishing they had not bestowed it upon you in the first place. "Why couldn't they have given it to Mr. and Mrs. Shootout? They love deer hunting! And why on earth didn't they give us cheese?"

Hush! Hush!

All of us have been given the gift of imagination in some measure. Most of us treat it like the butterfly in the glass case. We feel guilty because we realize it should be displayed. We have no doubt as to its value, but where or how to use it, we know not. The thing to do with useless gifts is to imagine some use for them and go ahead and use them. A record you didn't like makes a fabulous plant pot if melted and turned up at the edges! You can do it! Just use your imagination!

When Stuart traveled extensively and I stayed at home, I used to get many opportunities to preach in Methodist churches. Each Sunday I would deliver the finest message I could think of. But I had a problem. I didn't believe I could think of any fine messages of my own. I was far too insecure to use fresh illustrations that were of my own making, because I couldn't "imagine" being able to think of any better than other people had already thought up! I did have two sermons of my own which had taken me about two years to put together, but they got a bit boring to me after delivering them a few times. And I'll tell you something, if the preacher is bored with his material, think of the poor audience! So, I went around the north of England preaching Stuart's sermons! Needless to say, his sermons were grand!

In a brief interval, while home from his travels, my husband was invited to speak in a church in Manchester. I waved him off and began to get on with my domestic duties, when suddenly I went cold with dreadful anticipation. I had forgotten to tell him I had been to that particular church the month before and preached his fine sermon on Lazarus! I waited all day with a weight in my stomach. Sure enough, I needed no telepathy to tell me the worst as he walked in the door that night.

"You preached on Lazarus?" I whispered.

"Yes," he replied, "and a lady came up to me and told me I'd stolen your sermon." Then he added some words that had important repercussions in my life:

"Stop preaching 'my' sermons and go and find some of your own!"

"But I can't!" I wailed.

His answer was to tell me to put my coat on and take a walk with him. He made me "look" and "perceive" things around me. Then he made me create illustrations and think of applications of biblical truth. We leaned over a small bridge, and I dropped a pebble into the water beneath us.

"Which verse does that remind you of?" he asked me.

"Acts 1:8," I said, as I watched the ripple that began with the initial entrance of the pebble and widened until it encompassed the entire pool. "But ye shall receive power, after the Holy Spirit is come upon you: and ye shall be witnesses unto me both in Jerusalem, and in all Judea, and in Samaria, and unto the uttermost part of the earth." I was off and running.

I have discovered I do have an imagination—everyone does. Some, more than others, true; but all made in the imaginative God's image have some ability to creatively imagine. The Spirit of God will help us set that gift in a permanent place in the room of our thought processes and get it working. Pray about it!

Now I want you to try to "imagine" around a passage of Scripture. Choose one of the following, read the story, and then just sit and let your mind go.
1. *The call of Matthew (Matt. 9:9)*
2. *The Gadara demoniac (Matt. 8:28-34)*
3. *Jesus blesses little children (Matt. 19:13-15)*
4. *The rich young ruler (Matt. 19:16-26)*

5. *Peter's confession of Christ (Matt. 16:13-16)*
6. *A resurrection meeting (Matt. 28:1-10)*
Think about
    colors
    smells
    ·*sounds*
    atmosphere
    the appearance of onlookers
    the look on the participants' faces as they watch
        the action and the movements of the par-
        ticipants
Imagine, for example, what the blind man felt as he saw for the very first time—go on, imagine it! Feel it! Concentrate on that for a minute. Then, articulate your praise to God for it all!

S stands for Sing

Yes, sing. We discovered that the spirit of praise is a spirit of song! Music can lift our souls above the mundane into the realm of worship. Now everyone enjoys different types of music. After a beautiful organ recital my husband commented enthusiastically to our eldest son, "Did you notice how much the organist played on that organ with her feet?" "It sounded as if she played the whole thing with her feet" was the typical teen-age response! Organ music did not inspire our seventeen-year-old son to praise. That was made very clear to us! That week, however, the same son took part in "The Miracle Worker," a musical by Robert J. Hughes. I watched his face as he put everything into the Negro spiritual "They Hung Him on the Cross for Me" and saw musically inspired praise in action!

You know what music touches your soul. It will be different for each of us. Use it. Sit quietly and listen to music and think about God; or sing to Him. You needn't worry if you are in tune—remember He hears the crows as well as the nightingales!

Here are two praise choruses you might use together in your group or on your own:

"Alleluia!" by Gil Moegerle[1]

"Holy, Holy" by Jimmy Owens[2]

E stands for Express

Just tell God you love Him! Do you know how hard that is sometimes? For a husband to stop saying "I love you" to his wife may mean she will go and find someone else who will. God will never do that to us, but He loves to hear us tell Him we love Him.

In Revelation 2:4, the Lord says, "I have somewhat against thee, because thou hast left thy first love." One of the signs of a cooling-off relationship is a lack of verbal expression of our feelings. We can all say something as simple as, "I love You, Lord. I love You a little, Lord, but I'd like to love You a lot!"

Take time and tell Him now. Just "love" Him in prayer.

---

[1]*Hymnal for Contemporary Christians*, published by Singspiration Music.

[2]*Folk Celebration*, published by Singspiration Music.

Hush! Hush!

This is a pattern for praise you can follow using the ideas in the first chapter as well. Let me remind you of the acrostic:

P = Prepare
R = Remember
A = Adore
I = Imagine
S = Sing
E = Express

Hallelujah! What a Savior!

4

A Vision of Christ

Dear God,

I'm just beginning to figure out what it means to know You. I suppose that I'll always be figuring you out in all of my messy situations. I think I'm learning what it means to really know You as God and not as a person whom I want to be God. You're so much different than I am. But we have eternity for You to teach me to be like You. You are mercy and love to me.

Harold

4

A Vision of Christ

It's not difficult to see what God has to do with prayer. He is the One who has the wherewithal to deliver the answers. Yet Jesus Christ's part in it all is a little more difficult to understand. In fact, many people say it is not even necessary to bring Him into it. They say you can go straight to God without invoking the name of Jesus. But the Bible teaches us that we cannot just blast off into the very presence of God. We must not ignore the signs that instruct us to enter into that fantastic throne room in a prescribed way.

Not long ago I had to have some tests at the hospital. My doctor gave me a note, which I carefully clutched to me as I approached the gate. In his name I announced my arrival. There was no way I could obtain my conference with the surgeon without that note signed by my doctor's own hand. I was then instructed to follow a yellow line on the floor that would eventually lead me to the inner office of the specialist who would listen to my problem, diagnose the disease, and prescribe a remedy. I would never have tried to find my own way or take an unauthorized route. Neither did I think of throwing away the name of my doctor who sent me to the surgeon, with all of his authority behind that interview. I was in a different world. The medical world was totally strange and unfamiliar, and who was I to know better than the principalities who ruled that sphere? Following the instructions carefully, I arrived in front of the big man himself. He read my doctor's note, smiled, and gently began to ask me many questions. I was so scared and nervous. If only my doctor was there to be with me and explain my case. Suddenly the door opened and there he was! Knowing my justified fear, he had come himself to be with me.

Jesus Christ said, "I am the Way, the Truth, and the Life; no man cometh unto the Father but by Me." The note I hold in my hand has my disease on it—sin and selfishness. It is signed by my Jesus in His own blood; and, following His instructions, I approach the inner room where God is, the way He told me to—He said, "If you ask anything in my name, I will do it" (John 14:14). Therefore, in His name I come, and God receives me for His sake, for Jesus is none other than the second person of the Godhead. With all of His authority behind me, I dare to follow the arrows and find myself in a conference that begins to deal with my human malady. Feeling frightened in that inner place, I suddenly see Him—He is there to explain my case for me. What a relief! So you see, a vision of God is needed, but a vision of Christ is necessary too.

Because man's attitude toward prayer is often unbelievably arrogant, he needs to understand that he can't just saunter in "upstairs" any time he wants to. Even if he thinks God will almost fall out of heaven in His eagerness to grant his request and keep him happy, he has to be willing to have his ignorance exposed and learn some facts.

Now if we approach the High and Holy One with the attitude, "Here I am. I've come my own way, not Yours, and You'd better be grateful," I venture to suggest we've not had a true vision of God at all. If, on the other hand, we have begun to cultivate an attitude of intelligent praise, we will leave behind our small-minded ignorance and grasp God's relationship with Christ where prayer is concerned. Having begun to understand His character, we will then be overcome with a sense of awe-full-ness that results in our asking, "How can I possibly come near a Being as holy as this?" Apart from some authority who explains my presence and states my case, I will surely be tongue-tied, nervous, and extremely conscious of my unworthiness.

Maybe some of us, realizing all this and acquiescing to the brightness of His presence, feel we might better send our prayers via some super-saint, who could survive the proximity of holiness and deliver them for us. The more we come to know God, the more the concept of a Mediator—that is, someone who will stand in between us and God and speak on our behalf—becomes an obvious necessity.

Some of us go to the antithesis of arrogance and decide God is too busy to be bothered with such human trivia. Overconscious of our inadequacy, we bury our heads in our hands and duck behind the wooden church pew, whispering furtively toward the floor. We may wonder if some holy angel will find those needy words and bear them up, winging them toward the throne room—but we doubt it. How can He understand me anyway? If prayer is sharing my heart with someone who can understand my earthly problems, maybe it would be more practical to pray to another human being instead of a divine Spirit who does not know the feelings of the infirmities of my fallen humanity. Unless, of course, God could know what it is to be a man; then He would know how hard it is down here—"here" being the place I live, and struggle, and puzzle, and fail.

But that's what He did, didn't He? Became a Man, I mean. And that's what it's all about. We *have* a Mediator who lived on earth and now lives forever in heaven. There is a perfect human being in glory—His name is Jesus, our Savior and Intercessor.

Daniel saw Him in the very throne room with God. That vision must have given him a terrific shock. I'm sure whatever else he was expecting, he wasn't expecting to see a Man in heaven.

Look up Daniel 7:13-14 and write in your notebook or share in discussion a description of the scene in heaven.

The vision Daniel saw was a vision of One like a Son of Man receiving a kingdom, an eternal kingdom, from the hand of the Father. We know who that Man was, don't we? He was the preincarnate Son of God. What a priceless comfort to know there is a Man in glory.

In Exodus days God taught His people a very simple lesson. It was this—they would need a holy man, called a priest, to present their petitions to God. He would meet them at the door of the tabernacle and receive their sacrifice for sin and their prayer requests, then he would pray for them.

The tabernacle—God's graphic visual aid in the wilderness—was the meeting place for sinful man and holy God.

A Vision of Christ

There was a place within it called the Holy of Holies, which housed the law written on tables of stone. This was covered with the mercy seat. Here God had promised to meet with His people. The holiness of God required a careful approach into His presence. Instructions had to be followed, and the rules were meticulously given by God to Moses, who gave them to the people.

Once a year the great high priest was allowed to enter the "holiest of all," bringing with him the sacrifice for the sin of the nation. The sacrifice was in the form of a young and perfect lamb which had just been slain, prefiguring the Lamb of God who would take away the sin of the world. Blood would be sprinkled on that empty mercy seat, a reminder that a life must be shed if there was to be an "at-one-ment" between sinful man and holy God. Only by the shedding of blood could there be remission or forgiveness of sin. What sin? The sin of breaking those Ten Commandments of this holy God encased in the ark of promise underneath the mercy seat.

Even the way into the "holiest of all" was cut off from the sinner by a heavy curtain or veil. Now we know when the Lamb of God did appear to put away sin once and for all, by the sacrifice of Himself, that the veil was rent in two and a way was opened into the very presence of God. Presenting Himself to the Ancient of Days as the supreme and adequate sacrifice for the sin of the whole world, Jesus was accepted by the Father and He sat down on that empty mercy seat, which is His throne in heaven (Heb. 8:1-2). It is the place where justice and mercy meet for you and for me. It is the place where my Savior, both Lamb and Priest, sits to receive me for an audience with the King. The throne is close to the ear of God, and the Scriptures tell me plainly that He ever lives to make intercession for me. No longer do I need an earthly priest to take my prayer into God's

57

presence. I have Jesus, my great High Priest, who has passed into the heavens for me. Let us turn in the Scriptures and read about it.

> Read Hebrews 4:14-16. *Verbalize to the group or describe in your notebook what you think this is saying.*

There are four things that we can learn about the prayer work Jesus our great High Priest is accomplishing on our behalf. *First* of all, we know He *sympathizes* with us. How do we know this?

> Write in your book and discuss if in a group, Hebrews 5:1-2, and answer:
> 1. How do we know our Lord is sympathetic to us?
> 2. In your own words, sum up Jesus' feelings about us as found in Hebrews 4:15.

I always believed that Jesus was touched by my infirmities, but I never realized before that He was actually touched by the very *feelings* of my infirmities. Sometimes I really believe no one, not even those closest to me, can understand how I feel. I can try to explain, but the words don't come out right; and sometimes I don't even understand myself, so that I can explain me! I only know I suffer agonies no one seems to understand.

Now then, Jesus my great High Priest has been there because He was taken from among men. He can truly have compassion because He has "felt" my feelings. He knows; He cares; He understands. He is touched with the very feeling of my infirmities; therefore, I can come boldly to the throne of grace. And when I come to Him, what will He give me?

Well, *second*, we find we have a High Priest who *supplies*. Supplies what? Mercy and grace to help us in our time of need. What is the difference between mercy and grace? Mercy doesn't give us everything we deserve; grace gives us what we don't deserve.

Some time ago Stuart was explaining the difference between justice, mercy, and grace, using a helpful illustration. When Pete, our youngest, was small, he needed disciplining for a breach of family law. As he was asked to bend over, so Stuart could apply the board of education to his seat of learning, Pete said, "Hurry up, dad, 'cause I don't believe this is going to hurt you as much as it does me!" After five out of the prescribed ten whacks had been administered for the just reward of his deeds, dad stopped. "Why have you stopped, dad?" inquired Pete. "Because I have mercy on you," replied his father. "Justice gives you all you've asked for, while mercy doesn't give you all you deserve!" Pete went to his room to contemplate the proceedings, and soon his dad called upstairs to ask if he'd like to go for some ice cream with him. What was that? Well, that was grace. Grace gives you what you don't deserve!

We have a High Priest who understands us perfectly because He was tempted in every way we are, yet without sin. Therefore we come boldly to the throne room, knowing we will receive mercy. This is a sharp and true reminder of our sinful nature, yet grace to help with the repercussions of that deceitful heart of ours. This we don't deserve at all! So when my time of need comes, I know where my help can be found—in the throne room. Remember, God has given everything to His Son. In Christ are all the heavenly resources necessary to help me in my time of need. I will be supplied with a quality of divine help that is eternal. It never loses its value; it is called grace, and it is dispensed by the Son of God from the mercy seat in the "holiest of all."

Jesus Christ is the Source of the supply of grace. Look up John 1:17 and copy it into your notebook. The following verses tell us some of the things He supplies in grace. What does grace consist of? Write down the answers from each verse. If you are in a group, read them aloud, putting them into your own words.

Example: 2 Timothy 2:1: "Thou therefore, my son, be strong in the grace that is in Christ Jesus." Answer: He will supply strength, when I am weak.

1. *Ephesians 1:7; 2:5*
2. *Colossians 3:16*
3. *2 Thessalonians 2:16*
4. *Hebrews 12:28*
5. *2 Peter 3:18*

What was Paul's testimony?

1. *1 Corinthians 15:10*
2. *2 Corinthians 12:9*

Third, Christ is a High Priest who saves us. There are, basically, three aspects of our salvation: He has saved us from our sins, He is saving us now from our selfishness, and He will save us from judgment when we face Him in eternity.

Work on the following questions in pairs or in your notebook. Share your findings if in a class or group.

A Vision of Christ

1. Read Hebrews 7:23-26. What is the difference between our heavenly High Priest Jesus and an earthly human one such as Aaron?
2. What does Christ ever live to do for us (v. 25)?
3. How can we be sure God hears the prayers of our great High Priest (v. 26)?
4. In verse 25 we read a statement of His ability on our behalf. Verbalize it to your partner or write it in your own words in your notebook.

In the King James Version, Hebrews 7:25 says, "He is able to save them to the uttermost." As a street preacher once put it, He is able to save from "the guttermost to the uttermost." No matter to what depths we have sunk, no matter how great our need, or how fast sin or habit holds us, *He is able*. Not only is He able to save us to the uttermost, He is willing; and not only is He willing, He is praying to the Father on our behalf for our release. He longs to release the supply of strength and grace that we need in order to overcome. He waits for us to ask Him to do just that through prayer.

Lastly, Jesus is the High Priest who is *seated*. Where is He seated? Hebrews 8:1-2 tells us that He is seated on the right hand of the throne of the Majesty in heaven. He is our Mediator, the only One we need. We must approach God through Him, for the Ancient of Days has given Him the authority of the kingdom, and we can only be accepted in the Beloved.

Study together through these passages of Scripture. Discuss or make notes.
1. Read Hebrews 8:1-2. How is Jesus here described?

2. What was the earthly counterpart of the tabernacle in the heavens (Heb. 8:5)?
3. What was the Holy Spirit saying about the
   Holiest of All through this visual aid of the Old
   Testament (Heb. 9:8)?
4. If the high priest's work was to mediate to the
   Father for the people, then Jesus, our heavenly
   minister and Mediator, ever lives to do just that
   for us (1 John 2:1). If we want to find out just
   what He is praying for us, we need to look at
   Hebrews 8:8-13. Make a list of Jesus' prayer requests on our behalf.
5. Read Hebrews 10:19-25. These verses tell us that
   there are three things beginning with "Let us"
   that we need to do. Name them.

   a. v. 22
   b. v. 23
   c. vv. 24-25

Prayer Time. Let us stop and pray about these three
things.

This is perhaps new and difficult ground for you. Until
we come to realize there is a Man in glory, who is Jesus, our
great High Priest, who ever lives to make intercession for
us, we will never come boldly before the throne. When we
realize the veil was rent for us—the veil being His flesh
(Heb. 10:20)—then we know He cares and prays for us.
When we think about His prayers, we have to realize He is
desirous of saving us now—He died for that reason. But
also we realize He lives to save us now—He was raised for
that reason! I can come in His name and for His sake,
because of His saving work on my behalf; and I can come
knowing I shall be supplied from the throne room with
grace to help in my time of need.

Jesus is praying for us, this the Bible teaches. We have

learned some of the things He is praying. Now let me ask you a question: Is He seeing His prayers answered in your life?

A Time of Silent Prayer

Leader may quietly instruct as follows:

Be very still and come into the throne room. See Jesus, your great High Priest, there for you. Come boldly to the Father in His name. Thank Him that the veil of His flesh was rent for you. Ask what you will.

Remember, He sympathizes, supplies, and saves; and because He is seated in glory, He has the power to work on your behalf.

Thank Him.

Leave your request with God. Jesus will pray about it too!

5

Jesus' Prayers

Lord, You said,
"Behold, I Am the God of all flesh.
Is there anything too hard for Me?"
I tremble when You direct that question
    my way,
for You live in me.
My inner being
is Christ's home.
Why am I ever weak
when I can have Your strength?
Why should I fear
when You say,
"I Am with you always."
I would hide myself in You.
No longer I—but Christ;
No longer I—dear Lord.

                                    Mini

5

Jesus' Prayers

We are fortunate to have two prayers of our Lord recorded for us in John 17 and Matthew 26. They are not prayers He told us to pray, but actual accounts of the words He spoke in prayer on our behalf.

I suppose that to listen to a man's prayers is to listen to and see into the real person he is. One feels almost embarrassed at the privilege of hearing a man bare his soul before God. John 17 is an unbelievably beautiful and practical prayer that the disciples experienced on their behalf. Their time of defeat in Gethsemane seems all the more sad in light of it!

Apparently Jesus made a habit of praying aloud. This was not for His benefit, that He might corral His wandering thoughts, but for our benefit! How do we know this? Look up John 11:41-42. If His audible prayers are indeed for "the people who stand by," may we who stand by listening to the words of His prayers today believe God sent Him and place our confidence in His manifest willingness to answer prayer!

Jesus' Prayer for Himself

Turn to John 17:1-4.

1. Write down the two things Jesus was able to say He had accomplished in His life on earth (v. 4).

2. What was the work He had come to do (vv. 2, 3)? In the light of verse 8, do you think there could be any similarity between the work the Father gave Jesus to do and the work He has given us to do?

3. What was His prayer for Himself as He faced the final accomplishment of that work upon the cross (v. 1)?

4. How then, in the light of my Example, Jesus, should I be praying for myself?

Take a few moments to pray about that. (Note how long Jesus prays for Himself and contrast the time He spends praying for us! Surely on that particular night He could have been forgiven for praying for Himself. What an Example!)

Jesus Prays for Us

Jesus prays next for His disciples. "I pray for them: I pray not for the world, but for them whom thou hast given me; for they are thine . . . Neither pray I for these alone, but for them also who shall believe on me through their word" (John 17:9,20). (That's us!)

Write down the reason we need Jesus our great High Priest to pray for us (vv. 11a,14). Make a list of the things He prays for us from the following:

v. 11	vv. 21-23
v. 13	v. 24
v. 15	v. 26
v. 17	

Share your findings with the person next to you in the group. Then each one pray for the other about these things. Keep your prayers short.

These are the things your great High Priest is praying for you in heaven. May you derive much comfort from such praying, and may He see the answers to these prayers in your life.

Read John 17. Place the following headings over the appropriate portions of Scripture. (These headings are a summary of some of Christ's requests on our behalf.)

JUSTIFIED	SANCTIFIED
PURIFIED	SATISFIED
EDIFIED	UNIFIED
GLORIFIED	

Example:

"These words spoke Jesus, and lifted up his eyes to heaven, and said, Father, the hour is come; glorify thy Son, that thy Son also may glorify thee: As thou hast given him power over all flesh, that he should give eternal life to as many as thou hast given

JUSTIFIED

him. And this is life eternal, that they might know thee the only true God, and Jesus Christ, whom

---

> thou hast sent. I have glorified thee on the earth: I
> have finished the work which thou gavest me to
> do" (John 17:1-4).

Even in His final agony of prayer before the Crucifixion,
we find our Lord Jesus praying desperately for Himself,
and yet never able to divorce Himself from concern for His
beloved disciples. Oh, that we might learn such unselfish-
ness as we pray for ourselves!

> Read Matthew 26:36-38 — twice.

Can you imagine what it must be like to have God tell
you that He's feeling "heavy" and very depressed (v. 38)?
That in itself is mind-boggling. But then to be asked to
respond to the divine request, "Stay here and watch with
Me"! Surely His closest and dearest human friends would
gladly and willingly fall to their knees, vowing to keep
alert and responsive to His need. What a privilege to sup-
port the Son of God as He battled with the forces of hell that
were seeking to oppose His decision to die!

It is rather surprising therefore to hear the snores
emanating from verse 40! "But they were tired," you say.
True, but so was Jesus. Tired, loving, giving, healing,
caring, teaching, admonishing, and warning these men!
Do you ever get tired of telling people the same thing over
and over again when no response is forthcoming? There is
nothing quite so frustrating as seeking to move the un-
movable or shake the unshakable out of their compla-
cency. "Watch and pray; there's a cross tomorrow," the
Son of God had warned loud and clear that very night!

Jesus' Prayers

Spend a moment writing out the warnings Jesus gave His followers about His impending departure.

1. John 14:2-3
2. John 14:28-29
3. John 15:12-13
4. John 16:5-7
5. John 17:1,4

Read John 16:16-22. If in a group, discuss. For a few moments just sit and imagine Jesus' frustration at their incomprehension!

The problem with the disciples at this particular point in time was that they had no sense of ministry to Christ. The ministry of prayer on His behalf was requested of them by Jesus, and they simply snored their response. But don't be too hard on them. What about us? How many times do people who are depressed ask us specifically to pray for them? "Of course I will," we reply. And then we snore our way happily through their crisis hours! We need to think of Jesus' rebuke: "Inasmuch as ye have done it unto one of the least of these my brethren, ye have done it unto Me" (Matt. 25:40). Forgive us, Lord! If we could grasp the sheer privilege of "doing it unto Him," it would become a precious Gethsemane experience, enabling the oppressed to yield to the will of the Father and us to rejoice in the powerful ministry of supporting prayer.

It is interesting to note that Jesus engaged in prayer even when He did not feel like it. When we are depressed, prayer is not the likeliest of our chosen pastimes. J. Sidlow Baxter, speaking at a booksellers' convention, used the following illustration. He said that the times we feel least like praying, we must take "will" by the hand, leaving our emotions behind! Mr. Will and you must then pray. Day after day this discipline must continue until one day, one emotion may say to the other, "Come on, we're not going to stop them; we may as well go along!"

If Jesus had come to His decision of obedience via the dictation of His emotions, it may well have been a depressed and wrong decision! But Mr. Will and Jesus prayed together in Gethsemane and agreed to allow the Father's will to be done, even though the emotions were dictating otherwise. How great it is that we can *decide* to do God's will when it's the last thing in the world we *want* to do!

Some people tend to think of prayer as a rope attaching a huge ship to a little boat. They are the boat, and the big ship is God's will. They think the rope of prayer is to be used to pull the big ship alongside their little boat. This is against all natural laws, just as it is against all spiritual laws to say, "Not Thy will but mine be done!" Obviously, what has to happen as we pull on the rope of obedience in prayer is that the little boat draws alongside the big ship and sails wherever the big ship wills.

Jesus was depressed and tired as well. But even though He was tired, He was master of His physical body. I think we pamper ourselves dreadfully. "I must get eight hours sleep or I'm no good for the Lord," I heard a lady say not long ago. There are certain times in our lives when the cross must be faced, and no amount of physical strength will equip us for that challenge. Spiritual resources are needed. Surely Jesus required a good night's sleep before being crucified! You might think He would have just excused Himself from the party early, curled up on some moss under His favorite olive tree, and made sure He was ready for the challenge! But read the schedule of the hours preceding the Crucifixion and realize how tired Christ must have been before it had even begun.

1. *Read Matthew 26:40-41 and write out a sum-*

> mary of the Lord's attitude toward tiredness at
> this point.
> 2. Where do I stand on this issue? Am I too easy on
>   myself?

Next, Jesus links prayer with the overcoming of tempta-
tion.

> Write out a list of the things Jesus and His followers
> would be tempted to do in the next hours.

If Jesus needed that Gethsemane prayer time, it goes
without saying that we do! And we need it when the crowd
is singing hosannahs! Don't be deceived; crowds change,
and we don't know if there'll be a hostile group and a cross
tomorrow. There will be some opportunity to die to our
selfishness, that is for sure; and to overcome that test we
need to be prepared!

As I read this passage of Scripture, I cannot believe the
concern of the Lord Jesus! With all that He had on His
mind, He kept coming back to shake His dopey disciples
awake—all to no avail. Then it was too late. The crowd
was back; the hosannahs had gone, and in their place the
discordant notes of hatred and hostility were heard. We
see Judas approaching his Master in cold anger, giving
Him his kiss of death, and we hear Jesus' response:
"*Friend!*" Friend? Yes the Man who taught the Sermon on
the Mount was beautifully demonstrating His own revolu-
tionary teaching—"Love your enemies, do good to those
who hate you, and pray for those who despitefully use
you." Judas, Judas, why are you doing this? Friend! See
Jesus reaching out—this is what you do when you've
watched and prayed your way through to deciding the will
of God is all there is left to do!

73

Hush! Hush!

Now then, let us have a look at the sleepy students. Peter is on his feet. He has a sword in his hand. Peter has not watched and prayed, and the test has come. We see him fail it with a resounding *F*. Descending on Malchus, who appeared to have a very tempting cranium, Peter decided to make him into twins! That's what happens when you snore your time away. You don't "reach out" like Jesus, you "strike out" like Peter and do damage to the one you have been given the opportunity to love.

Maybe an unexpected incident in the "crowd" at the office turns their hosannahs into hostility. Maybe it is aimed at you! Do you say "friend"—overcoming evil with good? Or do you "cut off their ear" by an unkind, slashing remark? Does your self-defense mechanism spring into play as Peter's did, or are you concerned about the opposition's ear and soul, as Jesus obviously was? I wonder if Malchus' restored hearing affected his heart after Christ's merciful touch? We will know one day, won't we!

"Friend, *why*, oh why, have you come?" Jesus asked Judas. What a contrast to Peter's panic plunge! When and how did Jesus do it? He did it when He was tired and very depressed. He did it when He didn't feel like doing it. That's *when* He did it. He went on in importunate prayer, praying the same words until He had pulled Himself in agony alongside His Father's will. That's *how* He did it. He did it with a sense of ministry, honesty, and agony and demonstrated in jeopardy a sense of victory!

When Judas comes tomorrow, what will you call him? What will you do? It will all depend on what happens today in Gethsemane.

Read again Matthew 26:36-52. Place the following titles over the appropriate sections of text they describe. (These titles illustrate some of the sensitivity

Christ was seeking to teach His followers concerning their prayer life.)
Sensitive praying includes:

A SENSE OF MINISTRY

A SENSE OF AGONY

A SENSE OF HONESTY

A SENSE OF IMPORTUNITY

A SENSE OF JEOPARDY

A SENSE OF VICTORY

Example:

A Sense of Ministry

"And he took with him Peter and the two sons of Zebedee, and began to be sorrowful and very heavy" (Matt. 26:37).

Prayer Time. Pray about your daily "Gethsemane" experience or lack of it. Commit yourself to someone who needs you to "watch and pray" with him or her through their crisis hours. Prayer for self cannot be divorced from one's prayer concern for others.

6

Listening Through Your Eyes

I just want to thank You that little things don't seem foolish to You. Thank You for just revealing Your love to me. I want to thank You that You don't leave a prayer unanswered or a stone unturned. I thank You that You don't keep a record of the times I failed You.

How I praise You, Lord, for Your tenacious love. If I were You, I would have given up on this stubborn, bratty child (me) a long time ago. . . . But You didn't! The work of Your Spirit in me, though seemingly so slow, is so permanent! I love You, Lord!

6

Listening Through Your Eyes

Although it is far more important for God to talk to us than for us to talk to Him, it is helpful to clarify what He is saying by verbalizing a response. We used the three exercises that follow to teach three different methods of weaving Scripture into one's prayer life. What you are really doing is "listening" through your eyes! That's right, you read God's Word and then respond to it. This is, I believe, true conversational prayer. Often we think of conversational prayer as a monologue—me chatting conversationally to God! However, using the Scriptures this way, we can truly have a dialogue in a conversational way, which is what prayer is all about.

You may use these exercises individually in your own quiet time, or you may use them with your family or in a group or class. When we used them in class, I couldn't get anyone to stop! It came as a shock to me to realize that so many people who had known the Lord a long time had never taken the Bible simply as God's voice speaking to them—and had never given Him a verbal reply about what they were reading.

This is exciting—so, let's go.

Exercise One: The Pattern of Prayer

This lesson will show us how to take a short passage of Scripture and pray through it with this pattern of prayer. Split the group into twos and threes for this activity. This is the pattern:

> **P** raise
> **R** epentance
> **A** sking for others
> **Y** ourself

Example: John 14:1-6. Read passage through twice—once aloud, once silently.

1. **P**raise: *Share all the things you can praise God for from the passage (vv. 1,2,4-6).*
   Pause for Prayer
2. **R**epentance: *Can you find anything to repent about (vv. 1,5)?*
   Pause for Prayer
3. **A**sking: *What should you ask for others (vv. 1,2-3,6).*
   Pause for Prayer
4. **Y**ourself: *Ask for yourself. Discuss all the things you like about the passage. You need to pray for yourself.*
   Pause for Prayer

Other passages you can use this week are Psalm 1; Isaiah 5:1-7; John 15:1-8; Romans 8:26-39; Colossians 1:9-14; 1 Thessalonians 5:12-24; James 3:1-12.

Listening Through Your Eyes

Exercise Two: Bible Study Search*

Choose any passage of Scripture you like and use this quick Bible study search on it. Pray about it as you go.

Example: Read Philippians 4:4-13.
1. *Find the commands to obey. Underline them in green. Pray about them. Tell God about the ones you find difficult or even impossible!*
2. *Find the warnings in the passage. Underline them in blue. Repent in prayer about those you have not heeded. Ask God for strength to keep them.*
3. *Find the promises. Underline them in red. They are for you. Do you believe them? Talk to God about them.*
4. *Choose the verse you like best, the one that "speaks" to you. Write beside it why you like it or what it says to you. Talk to God about it.*
5. *Have a time of intercession on behalf of others through the warnings, promises, and commands you have discovered for yourself.*

Exercise Three: Verse by Verse

This is the most useful of all methods. It is the place Scripture and prayer meet and should be a natural thing for every believer. If you are in a group or in pairs, simply take a passage of Scripture verse by verse and person by person. Read your verse, put it into your own words, comment on it if you like, then pray aloud about it. Quite frankly, if I had done this every week with my present class of one hundred people, they would have been satisfied.

*You will need three colored pencils and a pen.

Hush! Hush!

Some suggested passages you could use:

> Psalm 27
> Proverbs 3:1-12
> Luke 6:27-42
> James 1:1-11

Let me illustrate how I have been greatly helped by this. Turn to Hebrews 4:7. Earlier in my life when I was a missionary, I found a big battle developing in my heart concerning the amount of time Stuart was away. I had grown cold and angry inside, but didn't believe anyone knew. (How could they help but know? After all, no one receives anything from you when you are out of touch!) After even refusing to look at the Bible for a short period of time for fear I would read something I didn't want to read, I deliberately began studying again. I started in Hebrews 4. When I arrived at verse 7, at once I was struck by reading twice in the same verse the word *today!* "Today's the day, Lord," I said. "Today I begin again to listen to You. I've shut my ears for so long, now I dare to open them again." But what was today to be for? Verse 7 says, "Today" if you will hear His voice, *"harden not your hearts."*

"My heart is so hard already, Lord, but I'll try not to harden it more," I responded. God then offered me rest from the struggle that had been raging in my life (v. 9). It was going to take effort on my part: "Let us labour . . . to enter into that rest" (v. 11). The effort would be the applying of my will to make a decision—the decision to yield! As I talked to Him about that, a strange thing began to happen to me. I found as always the Word of God was what it says it is—the *Word* of God to me! It was piercing my innermost being, discerning the very thoughts and intents of my heart. God knew my struggle and all its ramifications, and I knew I was not able to hide it from Him. As I read on in verses 12 and 13, I began to cry. Through my tears, I went on to read verses 14-16:

> Seeing then that we have a great high priest, that is passed into the heavens, Jesus the Son of God, let us hold fast our profession. For we have not an high priest who cannot be touched with the feeling of our infirmities, but was in all points tempted like as we are, yet without sin. Let us therefore come boldly unto the throne of grace, that we may obtain mercy, and find grace to help in time of need.

I talked to Him about that. I remembered He had to leave His home once for thirty-three years, so He could be "touched" with these feelings of my infirmities. He understood.

Then in a searing, convicting flash, I read in verse 15, "yet without sin." This brought repentance, more tears, a beating of my breast, and the cry, "God be merciful to me a sinner." A confession of my rebellion and a cry for mercy. There I found grace to help, and there my need was met.

Now I do not suggest a time of crisis before we search and apply the Scriptures! Every day the Lord Jesus and I read and talk together about the issues of life over His Word. We laugh together. I listen and ask questions, often reading on until I find His answer. This is the way I believe Scripture has its part in my prayer life.

I do not think it an accident that Hebrews 4:12, concerning the living, piercing Word of God, comes immediately before the invitation into the very throne room of God, where we are invited to discuss those imperatives, which, if obeyed, will make us like Him!

7

The Conditions of Prayer

Dear God,

I do have a lot of questions, and yet—*I don't listen to Your answers. . . .*

7

The Conditions of Prayer

If you purchase a cake mix and begin to put it together, I expect you will follow the instructions on the package. This way you will obtain the desired result. Conditions must be fulfilled if the cake is to look like the picture on the package. But if you decide to do it your way, and toss all sorts of things into the bowl, then you will find it just doesn't work. I'm sure you'll agree it would be rather foolish, to say the least, to blame the manufacturer for the failure! In the same way, the desired results of prayer can only be obtained if you fulfill the conditions. This is one good reason some prayers are never answered. We just haven't bothered to read the instructions.

But reading the instructions and discovering the conditions can prove to be quite discouraging for a Christian. The more conditions we discover, the more complicated it all seems to become! But don't stop praying! Think of it in the light of relationship. The earthly father receives many requests from his child. He often lays conditions upon the receiver. "If you do such and such, I will give it to you," he may say. Or he may want to know why you want the thing you are asking for. A good parent must consider many things. Will it benefit you? Are you too young to handle it? Can he see that the granted request would be far more of a blessing given at a future date? His answer may be *yes, no,* or *wait.* Whatever he withholds, it will surely be in love. Our own dear heavenly Father can be relied on to know what is best for us. And as we grow in our relationship with Him, we begin to understand why He withholds or refuses our petitions. We grow up enough to stop stomping our foot or screaming in rage as He apparently thwarts our desires. In other words, we come to understand the conditions of prayer. So keep praying *as* you grow in your knowledge of Him.

The Bible talks of many things that hinder our relationship with God. Negative attitudes may prevent God from hearing us. We may still be praying, but we realize He isn't hearing. Why? Let us look at some of these things.

Work in pairs or on your own with pencil, note-book, and Bible.

One negative condition is known sin in your life.

1. *Look up Psalm 66:18 and write it out in your own words. Also read Isaiah 1:15-16. To "regard iniquity" means to allow known sin to remain. An example in the Old Testament is found in the story of Achan.*

2. *Look up Joshua 7. If you are working in a group, it may be read in turn around the circle.*

Discuss the following questions:

   a. In verses 10-13, God commands Joshua to stop praying! Why?

The Conditions of Prayer

> b. What has Achan done that deserves death (v. 13)?
>
> c. How does God tell Joshua to find the culprit (vv. 14-15)?
>
> d. In verses 19-22 it appears Achan confesses. Why then punish him?

The main point of this Old Testament illustration is, I am sure, to teach us that to hide sin in our tents does not hide it from God, for "all things are naked and opened unto the eyes of him with whom we have to do" (Heb. 4:13). There is another obvious lesson to be learned. Sin in my tent, if allowed to remain, will affect the whole congregation!

To "regard iniquity" is to make sure my prayers remain unanswered, and you may as well get up off your knees and go and deal with it! Confess it. See the people involved, apologize, and "die" to it, even as Achan did.

So a bad relationship with your God, because of hidden sin, needs to be dealt with *before* you come to prayer. Always ask God to cleanse your life from known and unknown sin each time you pray. If it is known, forsake it as thoroughly as a dead man would, for "How shall we, who are dead to sin, live any longer in it?" (Rom. 6:2 *author's paraphrase*).

Other negative attitudes, which affect your prayers being speedily answered, are those that have to do with relationships within your family.

> 1. Paraphrase 1 Peter 3:6-7.
> 2. What did Jesus say about this: Matthew 5:23-24?
> 3. Write out and discuss 1 John 1:5-7.
>
> *Two more common attitudes that affect our prayers appear in the following verses. Look them up, write*

> them out in your own words, and then discuss them:
> James 4:2-3.

We have been quite negative up to this point. Now let us look at the other side of the coin. Negative conditions must be dealt with, but positive commands about prayer must also be fulfilled. First, let us look at *faith*—faith in a God we can come to who will reward us.

> Look up and read Hebrews 11:6. Write down your own interpretation of this verse. Then I will tell you what I think it means. Maybe we will come to the same conclusions!

When I first became a Christian, I thought if I had enough faith to believe God was as big and as great as His holy Word told me He was, then He would reward me. The reward would be the answer to my request, of course! I don't believe this any more. I most certainly have been rewarded every time I have come to my Father in heaven, trusting Him and acknowledging His ability to help or answer. But the reward has not always been the specific answer I asked for.

To encourage you to have faith in God through prayer does not mean God has to answer your prayer as you outline it to Him, when and how you desire. It does mean He will answer it His way, and He Himself will *be* your reward, whatever events happen to surprise you!

Do we have enough faith in the God we petition to tell Him our desire and accept the ensuing situations as His answer? Can we believe in the sovereignty of God enough to trust Him to carry us to the end of the journey all in one piece spiritually, if not physically, along a route *we* never gave Him permission to take us?

Years ago I rode a motorcycle. One day it refused to start. I left the machine locked up and boarded a bus to take me home. I was busy dreaming about my date for the evening, when the ticket collector inquired if I didn't trust the driver. "Why is that?" I asked, startled. Then I realized I still had my crash helmet on!

There are many crash-helmeted Christians today. They get on the bus of trust through prayer, but expect it to crash at any minute. We need to relax and allow the Driver to take us home by whatever route He chooses—even if it is unfamiliar or dark or spooky! You told Him your desired destination, now it is up to Him to take you there. So relax. Trust Him. *That* is reward indeed.

Often God rewards us with *more* than we ask. Sometimes we ask for a dime and He gives us a dollar. For example, we pray He will care for our children. We usually mean for Him to keep them safe physically. Yet sometimes He answers that prayer by allowing them to get hurt physically, that their faith may grow spiritually. To be "safe" spiritually *has* to be the greater reward.

God is, of course, interested and concerned about our physical growth and health. When I have to be away from home, I find myself worrying about my children. Sometimes it keeps me awake at night. Lying there in a strange bed, stiff with fear, I imagine everything that *can*, and I am sure *will*, happen to them while I am away. Reaching for the phone, I hear it ring—five times! By the time they answer it, I have already had the funeral!

"Oh, mum," I hear an impatient voice say, "what do you want? We are in the middle of a TV special!" I say good-by, but I still continue to toss and turn. One time, turning to my Bible, I read, "He that keepeth Israel shall neither slumber nor sleep" (Ps. 121:4). So God said to me, "There's no point in *both* of us lying awake. You sleep; I'll keep!"

Once I slept, and He didn't keep! Or did He? Judy went through a glass window, severing the main tendon in her wrist. Three thousand miles away, I accused God of breaking His promise. "You didn't keep," I sobbed. "You didn't, and I trusted You."

"Oh, but I did," He replied. "I kept her artery from being cut, thus saving her life. I provided her with instant medical expertise and a fine hospital to stay in."

"But I wasn't there," I wailed.

"I was," He replied. "I was her Reward, and now she is safer than she ever was before, spiritually safer, because she has learned I will be with her in whatever valley she must walk through."

And so I learned He rewarded my child with a far richer experience than I had asked for her, and rewarded me with strength to continue to serve Him thousands of miles away from my hurt little girl! His rewards come in strange wrappings tied with unexpected strings. We look for the familiar, the gift we explicitly ordered from heaven, and receive instead the beautiful surprise packages of God. They are always tied in love by those nail-pierced hands.

Work on the following together as a group or individually:

1. *Abiding is another positive condition.*

    a. Read John 15:7. Write out the promise it contains.

    b. Make a list of the conditions of abiding from John 15:1-17.

2. *Praying in His name, for His sake, according to his will:*

    a. Read John 14:13-14; 15:7,16; 16:23-24.

    b. Write out what you think it means to
pray in His name, etc. (Remember our lesson on
Jesus our great High Priest.)
    c. To pray for the right things we need the
help of the Holy Spirit, who will tell us what to
pray. Look up and read John 16:7. How would
you explain this to a child?
3. We must pray with thanksgiving. Learn Colossians 4:2 by heart.
4. We must be in earnest. Read James 5:7-18 and
   1 Kings 18:41-46. The word fervent means
   "stretched out."

You want the promised cake? Then read and follow the
instructions!

8

Praying for Our Loved Ones

Dear God,

I have prayed to You occasionally about Scott and how he believes there is a God, but he doesn't believe the things the Bible teaches. Lord, he is such a nice guy and I like him; but since he is an agnostic and I don't know what he believes or disbelieves, please send someone other than me to witness to him. Certainly, Lord, You know of better people than I to talk to him, for I don't know a thing about agnosticism. Besides, Lord, I am not a very good "witnesser." I might dishonor You in front of Scott and some of his friends. Lord, I don't want to do that—I want to honor You. Please help me!!

Your son,
Ken
(age 15)

8

Praying for Our Loved Ones

God loves our loved ones more than we do. It is through prayer that we come to this grand realization. If we do little praying, we will find ourselves subconsciously believing that even though God loves so-and-so, He cannot possibly love him as much as we do! This is understandable, we reason to ourselves. After all, I'm related to that person. He isn't. She's my wife; he's my son or daughter or boyfriend—therefore, I am in a better position to really care and understand. Prayer suddenly becomes a sort of protective layer we must use to shield them from an angry, judgmental God, whom we believe is not very pleased with their life style.

Communication with God about people involves our spending enough time with Him to enable us to understand how He really feels about those we love. If we will only talk it out in prayer and listen to His answers, we will make a remarkable discovery. We will find out that we are not more merciful, loving, and forgiving than God! We will discover we do not have to convince Him that our dear ones are not as bad as He thinks they are, and we do not have to remind Him of their good qualities. Neither need we explain the "reason" for their disobedience. We do not need to try to "protect" them from His dealings with them at all, for we come to understand that His dealings with them are in *love*. An all-seeing, all-knowing, all-merciful *love*.

Let me illustrate the release this brings to our hearts. We find we can trust God with those we love. To trust is to find rest from concern, not because we prayed for them and saw Him jump to our commands, but because in prayer we have "seen" the heart of God toward them and can never doubt again that He loves them more than we do.

Stuart spent the first seven years of our married life traveling. This put much responsibility on my shoulders. I was to be mother and father to our three lively children. When he came home, it was difficult for me to suddenly relinquish that authority role to him. I felt he didn't know our kids as well as I did, simply because he was not around enough to know them. Therefore, I felt his dealings in judgment would not be according to knowledge. I felt I must avoid confrontation between each child and his father, and so I would anticipate trouble and always be hovering around to intervene on their behalf. I did not talk this out with my husband, and so the attitude remained.

When God graciously gave us time together as a family after ten years of missionary work, I found the battle continued. Especially where our teen-age daughter was concerned. *How could he possibly understand her?* I reasoned. She was a woman; she was extremely strong-willed; and I could see confrontations developing every ten minutes. I exhausted myself "being around" to play the peacemaker. This went on until one day my husband sat me down and talked it out with me. He told me to get out of the way, because I was depriving him of a relationship with his own child. He too must be allowed to learn to know her. He was rightly hurt because I had not trusted him to handle her. The biggest thing I saw was his love for her. And even though I knew mistakes might be made, I also knew that love would be the key to judgment. The release from that responsibility was fantastic. I just physically removed myself from approaching situations and let them "meet." Meet they did, learn they did, and a beautiful relationship in love now exists between them. I trust my husband's dealings with our children, and the rest that results is a prize indeed.

This is what happens when you spend much time in prayer with God about those you love. If you identify with all this, you are in good company. Abraham felt the same struggle about Lot, as we see in Genesis 18:16-23. This passage of Scripture is not a grand example of Abraham's using prayer to change God's mind about his loved ones. It is a perfect example of God's changing Abraham's understanding of His mind. God's judgment was according to knowledge, tempered with grace, and demonstrated in loving concern and action on Lot's behalf. To "talk it out" is to spend time listening to the loving heartbeat of God toward those we care for most. Then we can make the best of discoveries: "God loves them more than I do!"

Read Genesis 18:16-23 together or on your own. Then write the answers in your notebook or discuss the following questions with the group.

  1. *What made God want to share His plans with Abraham (vv. 17-19)?*

2. *This passage raises serious questions. Read verses 23-33.*
3. *Was God right or "righteous" in bringing such terrible judgment?*
4. *Whatever God does has to be right. Because He is righteous, He cannot do anything wrong. Do we believe this?*

Look up the following statements about the character of God and let the group read them aloud: Genesis 18:25; Deuteronomy 7:9; 32:4; Revelation 15:3; 16:7.

Scripture claims God is always right in what He does; even if it appears wrong to us, it can't be because of His revealed character! Sin must be judged; it is terrible. Therefore, God is right to judge it. Sin cost God His Son's life. Surely that demonstrates how seriously God sees sin.

5. *How do we know God was careful that He had His facts straight (Gen. 18:21-22)?*

I have found myself pleading in prayer that God will not judge! Now I realize that this is a pretty stupid way to pray. He has to be what He is—perfectly just. The judgment of God means man has value—his actions matter; therefore, he matters! A child who is never punished feels his actions have no consequence. Nobody cares what he does; therefore, he believes that what he does doesn't matter. There is no one in more trouble than the person who feels that her or she has no value. No, what we *are* matters to God, and what we *do* matters to God. He examines us closely, coming near to see if it's as bad as He thinks it is. *It is!* "Your life shouts to heaven for the judgment of God."

Now in prayer we come to believe that *whatever* the Judge of all the earth does *has* to be right, because *He is* rightness. When you have met with God as Abraham met with Him—Abraham, who stood on a hilltop and watched the judgment of God fall on a city full of people—and can say, "It must be right," then prayer has accomplished something.

As I studied this passage of Scripture, I realized that God didn't need to get a closer look. He isn't short-sighted! It was for Abraham's sake that He came, so His friend might understand that He was willing, far beyond the requirements of mercy, to give Sodom yet another chance. Surely an angel visit would bring repentance! By the time Abraham had finished praying, he believed he could accept God's apparently harsh dealings with his loved ones. Remember, Abraham never did know Lot was saved! All he saw was the smoke! Maybe it was just as well he didn't know. Better to think him dead than to learn the end of his degraded life, involving immorality with his own daughters (Gen. 19:30-38).

We need to ask God to prepare us through prayer for the things He knows will be happening, that we may believe He will deal with our loved ones in whatever way seems right to Him. That's hard—it may mean seeing judgment fall. But we will have discovered in prayer and through experience that there will never be judgment without mercy.

So, then, can our prayers change God's mind about something He has decided?

1. What are the relevant statements in these passages: Isaiah 40:12-31; Romans 11:33-34; 1 Corinthians 2:16? Abraham didn't change an angry God's mind; God changed Abraham's mind about His being unjust.

2. Discuss what Abraham learned about God through his experience (Gen. 18:16-33).

101

Hush! Hush!

a. About His fairness (v. 21).
b. About His grace (v. 26).
c. About speaking to a Holy God (vv. 27, 30,32).
d. About God's generosity (v. 32).

God loves those we love more than we do. He wishes to convey to us His care for those we love. Pray about it—now!

Make a list of all your loved ones. Decide if you believe He loves them more than you do. Then write a letter to God telling Him what you feel about them and also what you have learned through the story of Abraham about what He feels for them.

9

More Exciting Prayer Meetings

Dear Lord,

You know I have so much trouble getting up in front of people unless I really have confidence in myself and know that I am good or am impressing someone. It's all pride, I know, Lord. I just don't want to be lowered in anyone's eyes. But really, what does it matter if I'm eloquent or great in front of people. I'll be what You want me to—*that's all I ever can be anyway.*

Sarah

9

More Exciting Prayer Meetings

Some of the most boring times of my Christian life have been spent in church prayer meetings. Some of the funniest times of my Christian life have been spent in church prayer meetings. And some of the most blessed times. What makes the difference? What ingredients are needed to turn a prayer meeting from a "bane" into a blessing?

First of all, we have to learn to deal with Mrs. Mumbler. Off she goes, mumbling and bumbling. Her head is down, and her words are shooting straight into the shag carpet. All of us are nearly falling off our chairs in an effort to hear. It wouldn't be so bad, but she goes on and on; and then just when there's a pause and someone thinks it's all over, off she goes again, to the great embarrassment of the unintentional interrupter.

There is only one way out of this. As leader of the group, tell everyone (looking straight at Mrs. Mumbler) that we

105

will keep our heads up to pray, speak loud enough for all to hear, and if anyone prays too softly, you will stop the pray-er and ask for more volume.

Next, you may have a Mr. Got-to-tell-you-all-I-know in your group. This is a man who can't wait to impart his scriptural knowledge to the people in the prayer meeting. The scripture phrases flow on and on, as we trace the journeys of the children of Israel through the wilderness into the Promised Land, listen to the various prophets (were there really that many?) thunder their exhortations, and finish up with a quick survey of New Testament theology. When he eventually stops, everyone is so stunned there is a loud silence which he mistakes for appreciation!

Then there is Miss Steal-everything-there-is-to-pray-about-before-*you*-get-a-turn. This young lady really *is* a menace. You carefully enumerate the prayer requests. You can see one or two eager, but shy, young people who have come for the first time, and you want to give them plenty of items to choose from. Then Miss Steal-everything starts. She uses up every item on the list and ends with a triumphant, "So, Lord, continue with us as we pray on." Little Miss Frightened-out-of-her-mind sitting next to her is, of course, left with absolutely nothing to say. She has sat there in horror as item after item was used up, her mind frantically trying to think of some other petition. That is the way to make sure she never comes back again! As leader, you *must* make sure you ask the group to pray for only one or two requests at the most.

Then you have Mrs. Can't-wait-to-tell-you-all-the-juicy-gossip-I-can't-tell-you-with-my-eyes-open! This is an obnoxious lady who uses the public prayer meeting to pass on juicy news—all under the guise of praying for poor so-and-so. "Help Mrs. H. to know she mustn't have an affair with a married man now that she's a Christian," she prays in a hushed, sad monotone.

Now this *has* to be stopped, and I suggest that you, the leader, tell the group no names or situations must be revealed unless the item to be prayed about is common knowledge. The public prayer meeting was never intended to be a place to reveal private scandals.

Then there is Mr. Correct-your-prayer. He is the one who listens to a "starter prayer" and feels it his duty to catch the prayer in midair, sort in out, and deliver it as he knows it was intended to the Almighty! He is really doing the Holy Spirit's job, which is to sort out all our prayers and present the essence of them before the Father.

What do you do with the noisy pray-ers? Now, *amen* and *hallelujah* are scripturally proper in such places as a praise meeting, but what is important is consideration of others in the group, who may be disturbed by the noisiness of the amens. Furthermore, I have been in prayer meetings when amen—which means "so be it"—was added in ridiculous fashion to all sorts of statements.

Thank You for keeping us safe, Lord. . . . Amen!
Thank You for food and clothing, Lord. . . . Amen!
Thank You for healing Mrs. T, Lord. . . . Amen!
I've beaten my wife this week, Lord. . . . Amen!
Hallelujah!!!

We must intelligently articulate our "so-be-its" at the right times only if they will edify and unify the group, and if they do not cause uneasiness or division.

"How good and how pleasant it is for brethren to dwell together in unity" (Ps. 133:1).

The leader should pray about all these problems, be brave enough to approach the offenders in love and talk with them, and also plan a variety of prayer meetings using different formats to encourage new prayers and curtail long ones. A planned format is helpful to correct many of these problems.

As an exercise in our groups as we studied corporate prayer, the members worked out a planned format of a prayer meeting. Some examples appear later in this chapter, many of which we have used in our own prayer times. You may like to use one or more of them in yours. We put people into pairs to work out a thirty-minute prayer time. Maybe you, too, can put some formats together. You could collect them, place them in a file, and then recruit leaders who would use them in your church.

Corporate Prayer

Work together answering the questions and discussing the gathered information.

What the Bible Says

1. What is the minimum size for a corporate prayer meeting (Matt. 18:19-20)?
2. What is the maximum size (Acts 2:41-42; Rev. 19:1-6)?
3. When we come together, the atmosphere should be one of: confusion, variety, peace, criticism, edification, order, frenzy, decency, noise, unity. (Read 1 Cor. 14:26,33,40 and circle the right words.)
4. Read the account of Peter's miraculous release from prison in Acts 12:5-17. Discuss the following questions.
    a. How hard was the church praying (v. 5)?
    b. What effect was their prayer having on Peter in prison (v. 6)?
    c. How did he know where the church would be (v. 12)?

    d. Do you think Rhoda was expecting Peter (vv. 14-15)?

    e. Was the church expecting an answer to their prayers (vv. 15-16)?

    f. What does this story remind us about corporate prayer on behalf of our brothers and sisters in prison for their faith?

    g. What defects did this particular corporate prayer meeting appear to have?

    h. What good things were happening as a result of this prayer meeting?

Application

1. Make a list of the do's and don'ts to be observed in a prayer meeting.
2. Working in pairs, plan a half-hour prayer meeting for your church or group. Use all the ideas you have learned about.
3. Go to your pastor and ask if you can help with the prayer meeting. (Pick him up after he has fainted with shock and assure him you mean it.) After all, you really have no alternative but to obey the commandment of the Lord, who said, "When you pray, say . . ."

How to Pray for the Church

To inform the class about the needs of the fellowship, we invited several officers of our church fellowship to come and share their needs with the people. Dividing the large group into smaller units, we put an officer with each group for fifteen minutes. For five minutes they shared and for five minutes the group asked questions. For the last five minutes they prayed about those requests. We had a tremendous response to this. The officers were delighted, and the pray-ers were thrilled the very next week to hear about the answers to their intercessions.

As an example, our caretaker had been asked to share his problems, and he communicated the need for a student helper to clean the church building in the evenings. They had tried for weeks to find one but had not been successful. The little groups prayed, and the next week Mr. T. returned to ask if he could share the results. *Two* students had applied for the job that very week, and they had employed the one who appeared most suitable!

Other people you could invite to share could be:

Head of nursery	Sunday school superintendent
Caretaker	Youth leader
A deacon or elder	Member of church finance committee
Your pastor	Sound systems technician
A hospital visitor	Taping ministry representative
Office personnel	Missions committee representative

If you are endeavoring to do this study on your own, you can personally approach each one and become fully informed as to your church's prayer needs. You could also invite them to the church prayer meeting to explain their prayer needs. Have one of these persons sit in each group as they discuss the various Scriptures. Then have the group pray specifically for that person.

1. Caretaker: This person is responsible for the protection and maintenance of a great variety of things in the church (2 Kings 23:4; 1 Chron. 9:26-33; Ps. 121:3-4). His qualities are to be:

   (a) _____

   (b) _____

   (c) _____

2. Deacon or Elder: These men are to "serve tables" and

"teach" if needed (1 Tim. 3:1-13; Acts 6:1-6). Their character is to be:

(a)_____ (d) _____

(b) _____ (e)_____

(c)_____ (f) _____

3. Pastor: The pastor is to possess the qualities of a deacon or elder as well as those of a shepherd. What are the qualities of a shepherd (Ps. 23)?

(a)_____ (d) _____

(b) _____ (e)_____

(c)_____ (f) _____

4. Missions Committee: This busy and functional arm of the church is an extension over the world in a material as well as spiritual way. They need (Luke 22:32; John 4:35-36; Eph. 6:19; Col. 4:3):

(a)_____

(b)_____

(c)_____

5. Youth worker: Timothy is a living example of youth in the Bible. His spiritual father, Paul, encouraged him and probably prayed for him in these areas. List as many as you can find from 1 Timothy 1:18-19 and 2:11-16:

(a)_____ (d) _____

(b) _____ (e)_____

(c)_____ (f) _____

6. Music Committee: Music is a means of worship, praise, and expressing our emotions to the Lord. We are to sing with (1 Cor. 14:15):

   (a) _____

   (b) _____

   Therefore, we should pray _____and

   _____ for our music committee.

Paramount in our prayer life is thanksgiving for those Christ has chosen to serve Him in the church. Consider Paul's deep prayer in Philippians 1:3.

The following are testimonies to the value of this particular lesson:

> After hearing about those in the nursery who were unable to attend church for months, we were convicted! It's easy to say, "How sad! why doesn't *someone* do something?" We are "someone"—and have been soaking up church *and* Sunday school—so, in place of Sunday school next quarter, we'll take on the two-year-olds. Pray for us.

> One thing that had a great impact on me was the visit of a pastor to share the needs of his family, especially his children. Their identity and resentments about being "pastor's kids"—the pressures they had from their peers in school and church—impressed me to pray!

> Having the different group representatives talk to us was very special to me. It made me more aware of the desperate needs that fellow Christians in our own church are experiencing. It gave me insight into the fact that our leaders also need prayer and guidance and that they are not perfect. They have problems with spirituality too!
> It also made me feel as if I had been sitting too long being

"fed" by this church, and it was about time to start "feeding" others through what I have learned from being in this church.

The prayer index-card system is fantastic. I have started the system and, in the process, I have really gotten closer to people. Nothing impresses another person more than asking him if there is something that I could pray for him about—and actually write the request on a card in front of him. It shows a real witness of caring.

The Prayer Calendar/Card File

One of the members of our church brought a helpful "tool" along to share with us. The discovery of this simple tool has been helpful to me in maintaining an exciting, consistent prayer life. When mixed with discipline and a desire to be taught by the Holy Spirit, it enables freedom and flexibility to permeate a prayer calendar.

The tangible articles necessary to begin are a pack of three-by-five cards, a card file, and a pen. The operative tool will consist of cards with individual prayer reminders appropriately filed on a daily or weekly basis. This tool will help us in our personal prayer life, but one also may be kept at the prayer meeting for the use of the fellowship.

In order to establish a series of cards distinctive to yourself, begin by asking the Holy Spirit to make you sensitive to the needs of which He would have you aware. As people and/or ideas come to mind, start a card by marking an appropriate heading and noting the date and thought. For example, the life style of my friend John, who is not a Christian, has been abruptly affected by the discovery of metastatic cancer. The burden on my heart is that he come to know the Lord Jesus. My card for him begins:

John
9/2   *Crisis* $\longrightarrow$ *Salvation*

Remember:

—The cards are tools, not burdens; keep them simple.
—The cards are personal between you and God; no one
   else needs to understand them.

When you have established a card for each need of which
you are aware, sort them into daily and weekly categories
according to urgency and depth of need.

Remember:

—It is more effective to pray fervently once a week than
   to read off a list of names daily.
—Cards can be transferred from weekly to daily or vice
   versa as needs change.
—Keep a supply of blank cards; new needs will appear.

Make some dividers for your card file with headings
DAILY, MONDAY, TUESDAY, etc. Then each day as you pray,
you will consider the pack of daily cards and the pack of
weekly cards for that day.

The card will serve as a reminder and will also give
opportunity to keep a progress record. As you discuss with
God, on an ongoing basis, the specific need of which the
card reminds you, you will receive new insight and observe changes which will be too exciting not to record. A
new date is then noted with a new entry.

One of my most precious cards records for me my sister's

salvation experience. The entries reveal my concern for her in her relationships with others and her need for a relationship with the Lord Jesus Christ.

Name
*7/10 need for Christian friend. 8/5*_____
*8/26*_____ *10/1 moved in with Christian roommate!! 10/1* _____ *10/15 Conviction.*
10/15 Commitment!!!! 10/24 _____ *. etc.*

As you develop your prayer file, you will want to make adaptations that will effectually gear this tool to your personal needs. You may want to develop a "praise card" and observe the changing character of your praise to God as you grow in your relationship with Him. You may want to develop a very secret "repent card" and observe your progressive awareness of areas of darkness in your life as you continue to expose yourself more and more to His light. You may want to record scriptural promises or prayer models specific to your situation. Be creative!

Regardless of individual adaptations, however, a common privilege will be enjoyed. Namely, the opportunity to flip through your old cards from time to time and reflect on the miracles!

Some Sample Formats for Prayer Meetings

These were put together by groups in our prayer class. Your class can do this too!

Format Number One

1. Leader: Begin group session with a short prayer for guidance and open hearts.

a. Have a silent prayer and meditation time, fixing minds and thoughts on God.
b. Explain a simple definition of prayer and locate several areas in Scripture where prayer is mentioned.
c. Mention different types of prayer: (1) Praise, (2) Repentance, (3) Asking for others, (4) Asking for self.

2. General prayer time—following the above format.
3. Ask the group conditions for prayer, citing examples in the Bible.
4. Share personal answers to prayer.

Format Number Two: Praise, Petitions, Prayer

First 10 minutes: a song of praise and thank-you testimonies.

Next 10 minutes: prayer requests for missionaries, for the church, and for things mentioned by those present.

Last 10 minutes: fervent prayer by each one present for the things mentioned and other personal problems.

Format Number Three

1. Begin with a few minutes of fellowship:
   a. Praise song
   b. Sharing from personal lives
2. Organize prayer requests and assign them to individuals.
3. Pray, using a psalm to praise God. Each member of the group can say a verse out loud.
4. In pairs, pray for requests shared.
5. Pray with prayer partner about your own personal requests.
6. Close with sentence prayers of thanksgiving.

Format Number Four: For Health of the
Church Fellowship

Jesus calls us to prayer: Leader reads Matthew 11:28-30.
Praise: A member reads Psalm 111:1-3.
Prayer for guidance: Members read Psalm 16:7-8; 43:5;
    Isaiah 30:21. Others may add their own prayers.
Making things right: Members read John 15:12-13; Ro-
    mans 12:14-21; and James 5:16. Others may add their
    own prayers for members of the body of Christ and for
    specific needs.
Close: Leader gives thanks and then asks others for prayers
    of thanksgiving.

Format Number Five (1 hour)

A. *Call to order* (5 minutes)
    1. Leader opens with prayer
    2. Group in silent prayer
        a. Commit time to Christ
        b. Repent for loss of fellowship with Christ
    3. Leader closes
B. *Praise God* (20 minutes)
    1. For what He has done (Gen. 1:26-30)
    2. For what He will do (Rev. 22:1-5)
    3. Thank God for giving you a chance to talk with Him
        (Matt. 27:51; Mark 15:38; Heb. 4:14-16)
C. *Pray for God's will to be done by the pastoral staff* (10
    minutes)
    1. That God will strengthen them
        a. In Spirit
        b. In dedication and knowledge
        c. In physical strength and health
    2. For staff families

D. *Pray for fellowship* (10 minutes)
  1. To strengthen
      a. Tolerance of each other
      b. Commitment to Christ
  2. For commitment to help the church
      a. Recognize their spiritual gifts
      b. Commit gifts to church
E. *Pray for your needs* (15 minutes)
  1. Physical and spiritual
  2. Other personal prayer requests

Format Number Six: "Praise" Prayer Meeting Schedule

1. Leader: Greeting
          Read psalm of praise.
2. Split up into groups of four.
3. Quiet time for personal repentance.
4. Share what God is doing in individual lives and proceed to praise God in prayer.
5. Open to the Book of Psalms and share verses of praise and glory to God.
6. Large group together for time of praising God for who He is, what He does, His qualities. . . .
7. Time of fellowship.

Format Number Seven (1 hour)

Leader begins in prayer, using the pattern of prayer:
  1. Praise
  2. Repentance
  3. Asking for others
  4. Asking for yourself

Leader: Any passage of Scripture may be prayed through with this pattern of prayer. Let us get into small groups. Here is a sample passage: Psalm 1. Read passage through twice—once out loud, once in silence.

1. Share all things you can praise God for (vv. 1-3,6).
    Pray.
2. Can you find anything to repent about (vv. 1-3)?
    Pray.
3. Asking for others, as this passage applies to them (vv. 1-6).
    Pray.
4. Asking for self. Discuss your needs that have been brought to mind by this passage.
    Pray.

Leader: Remember that there are conditions to prayer, and if negative conditions prevail in your life, prayer will remain unanswered and unrewarding. *Sin in your tent affects the whole congregation* (Josh. 7:1-26)!

As time permits, choose a favorite passage of Scripture and pray through it with the "pattern for prayer."

Format Number Eight (30 minutes)

A. Ground Rules
1. Have hosts and hostesses make everyone feel welcome as they arrive.
2. Be informal, and keep people close together, not scattered throughout house, auditorium, etc.
3. Have a leader in each small group who will be able to pray and make others feel relaxed and at ease enough to pray.
4. Have a definite starting time. Don't get carried away chatting.

B. *Organization*

1. Leader opens meeting for a time of sharing: answered prayer, ways God is working, etc.
2. Sing. Leader leads a prayer of thanksgiving and opens it up for prayer requests.
3. Split into small groups of 3 to 5 people. Divide prayer requests among groups.
4. Time for sharing of more individual prayer requests.
5. Prayer, with a time limit.
6. Close with time of fellowship and plans for next meeting.

Format Number Nine

1. Choose topic—e.g., world affairs.
2. Leader: opening prayer.
3. Participants discuss different events from newspaper articles, broadcasts, etc.
4. Break up into groups of two or three to pray, each taking a specific subject mentioned.
5. Either come back to the large group or stay in small groups for concluding prayer time.

Format Number Ten

1. Leader could open with:
   a. Singing
   b. Sharing of what God's been doing
   c. Spontaneous Scripture reading
2. Prayer
   a. Praise
   b. Bless the needy
   c. Pray for our enemies and those we have trouble loving
   d. People in authority over us

   e. Increased faith

   f. Availability to God for His will

3. End by splitting into pairs, sharing one personal need or request with each other, and committing yourself to pray for that person all week.

Collecting Prayers

Another way of encouraging prayer is to suggest the group collect other people's prayers and make them their own. Our class enjoyed doing this. Here are a few examples they brought in. We added them to our file to be used if anyone so desired.

"O Lord, Almighty God of our fathers, Abraham, Isaac, and Jacob, and of their righteous seed; who hast made heaven and earth, with all the ornament thereof; who hast bound the sea by the word of thy commandment; who hast shut up the deep, and sealed it by thy terrible and glorious name. . . My transgressions are multiplied, and I am not worthy to behold and see the height of heaven for the multitude of mine iniquities. I am bowed down with many iron bands, that I cannot lift up mine head, neither have any release: for I have provoked thy wrath, and done evil before thee: I did not thy will, neither kept I thy commandments: I have set up abominations, and have multiplied offences. Now therefore I bow the knee of mine heart, beseeching thee of grace. . . ."

> Manasseh, King of Judah,
> when he was being held
> captive in Babylon

Hush! Hush!

O to grace how great a debtor
  Daily I'm constrained to be;
Let that grace now, like a fetter,
  Bind my wandering heart to thee.
Prone to wander, Lord, I feel it,
  Prone to leave the God I love—
Take my heart, O take and seal it,
  Seal it for thy courts above!

J. I. Packer,
Knowing God

from the hymn "Come, Thou Fount of Every Blessing"
written by Robert Robinson, 1758

Slow Me Down

Slow me down, Lord, I'm going too fast;
I can't see my brother when he's walking past.
I miss a lot of good things day by day.
I don't know a blessing when it comes my way.
Slow me down, Lord; I want to see more of the things
That are good for me.
A little less of me and a little more of You.
I want the heavenly atmosphere to trickle through.
Let me help a brother when the going's rough;
When folks work together, it ain't so tough.
Slow me down, Lord, so I can talk with some of Your
    angels.
Slow me down to a walk.

Unknown

"Father, I want to know Thee, but my coward heart fears
to give up its toys. I cannot part with them without in-
ward bleeding, and I do not try to hide from Thee the terror

of the parting. I come trembling, but I do come. Please root from my heart all those things which I have cherished so long, and which have become a very part of my living self, so that Thou mayest enter and dwell there without a rival. Then shalt Thou make the place of Thy feet glorious. Then shall my heart have no need of the sun to shine in it, for Thyself wilt be the light of it, and there shall be no night there."

A. W. Tozer
The Pursuit of God

Answer To Prayer

We ask for strength and God gives—
Us difficulties to make us strong.

We pray for wisdom and God sends—
Us problems,
The solution of which develops wisdom.

We plead for prosperity and God gives—
Us brain and brawn to work.

We plead for courage and God gives—
Us dangers to overcome.

We ask for favors and God gives—
Us opportunities.

This is the answer!

Hugh B. Brown
With Gratitude

Heavenly Father, I rejoice that this day has made me conscious of Thy presence. Thou hast led me to the end of

Hush! Hush!

it; Thou hast delivered me from many temptations. With gratitude, I come this hour. Let me bring cheerfulness and hope to those I meet tomorrow. In all I do or say, help me to be guided by Thy love. For Jesus' sake. Amen.

John T. Sandelin,
Boy's Book of Prayers

Almighty and most merciful Father; We have erred, and strayed from thy ways like lost sheep. We have followed too much the devices and desires of our own hearts. We have offended against thy holy laws. We have left undone those things which we ought to have done; And we have done those things which we ought not to have done; And there is no health in us. But thou, O Lord, have mercy upon us, miserable offenders. Spare thou those, O God, who confess their faults. Restore thou those who are penitent; According to thy promises declared unto mankind in Christ Jesus our Lord. And grant, O most merciful Father, for his sake; That we may hereafter live a godly, righteous, and sober life. To the glory of thy holy name. Amen.

The Book of Common Prayer

10

Praying for Ourselves

Dear God,

As You already know, I'm getting impatient with this present situation. I want, I want, I want; but what do You want? Please show me and teach me everything I need to learn from this time on in my life. Make me sensitive to Your leading and faithful enough to follow. Your little sheep,

Dave

Dear God,

I don't know how to go about doing the job You have given me. I am afraid even though You have promised to be with me. I don't know how to talk about You to my husband and to our sons. I have turned them off and don't know how to turn them back on.

If this is my job, please show me the way. Put the words in my mouth and the willingness in my heart to do Your will.

Liz

10

Praying for Ourselves

"Pray for me, mum." Pete bounced off the bottom step and onto the sidewalk as he issued his directive. He was on his way to start another school year with new hopes and dreams, new incentives, new goals. "Sure, Pete," I replied. "What for?" His answer took me aback. "I want first-chair clarinet," he announced. "But, Pete," I remonstrated, "I can't pray *that* for you—you haven't practiced in three months!" "Well," he replied looking mildly perturbed, "if I'd practiced, I wouldn't need *you* to pray!" I decided it was time to talk to Pete about prayer!

Some of you reading these pages want first-chair Christian. That's a great and noble goal. I would encourage you in your eagerness for the necessary holiness of life that sets you apart from the defeated fifty-first-chair disciple! But you can't have first-chair Christian overnight; just as you can't have first-chair clarinent without practicing for three months. That's the word—*practice!* It means going at a difficult set of circumstances from every possible way until you have mastered it. First-chair clarinet conjures up certain words to my mind—words like *time, effort, discipline, stickability, determination,* and above all *instruction from a master!* First-chair Christian brings to mind similar ideas.

Many people believe prayer is a magic wand; they expect to wave it to and fro in God's face and be changed from Cinderella into the princess. All they have to do is pray and God will give them the things they don't deserve.

Now God always *does* give us things we don't deserve, for if He gave us what we *do* deserve, we would all be crucified! But prayer, someone has said, is simply the "debating chamber of the soul." Here a subject is brought up for debate by the Master, and a frank and open discussion of all aspects is intended to take place. The subject is chosen carefully by God. Let us return to our analogy of master musician and pupil. God is not interested in producing by magic a finished symphony. He intends the pupil's character to be "finished" as he works on the Master's instructions and practices faithfully whatever skills are set for the lesson of the day.

The Master instructs, and we practice. He chooses the piece of music. We play it. Instead of trying to use prayer as a briefing time for the Almighty, telling Him to "magic up" some nice conclusion to a sticky situation we have brought upon ourselves; prayer should become a briefing time for us to hear how we can bring about our own conclusions! Prayer isn't telling God to practice something, but it is Him giving us our homework! If we give Him half a chance to get us alone regularly, He will change us and work with us that we may become the answer to our own prayer. Prayer is our opportunity to receive instruction that may require *action* on our part.

Now, to recapitulate: You remember praise gives us a vision of God, which leads to a vision of self and a vision of others, and then demands availability for action! "Here am I, send me" is the grand conclusion of praise (Isa. 6:8). Sometimes our service of inadequacy is so overwhelming that we become overawed at the command received in prayer, and so we protest instead of yield. Like Moses we say, "Here I am, send Aaron!" Or, like Jonah, we don't say anything at all.

Do you remember the story of Jonah? He was in prayer about the Assyrian people. They had been harassing Israel; and Jonah, a patriotic, nationalistic-minded Jew, was busy feeding the hatred in his heart toward his country's enemies. I'm sure he was demanding that Jehovah wipe them off the face of the earth. Instead, God told him to go and preach to them that He might have a chance to forgive! This way Jonah could become the answer to his own prayer. Nineveh would repent and get off Israel's back. You see, God is utterly committed to answering our prayers *His way!* But His way was not a way Jonah was ready to accept. Jonah's quiet time came to an abrupt halt. There was no way prayer could continue when the presence of the Lord meant obeying a command like that!

It is in prayer that we will find the will of God, but to find God's will is not necessarily to find ourselves willing to *do* it. If we continue in prayer, debating the issue until we can say as Jesus did, "Nevertheless *not* my will but thine be done" (Luke 22:42), then the purpose of prayer is accomplished; but if we say instead, "Not Thy will, but *mine* be done," we have no alternative but to do as Jonah did and "flee from the presence of the Lord." What is your Nineveh? What are you running away from as fast as you can go?

> *Spend a few moments right now in quiet contem-
> plation and answer that question. It helps to identify
> Nineveh. Then you must face it.*

What I love about the attitude of God toward Jonah is the
unavoidable inference in the story of God's great concern
for His prejudiced prophet! Even though Nineveh must be
given a chance to repent—for God is an internationalist
and longs that *all* should be saved—His concern was also
for the blessing of His angry, resentful servant! God was
about to manifest His power in many miraculous events in
these chapters, but the greatest miracle was to be the
changed heart and attitude of Jonah. He needed to repent
as well as Nineveh, and God intended to give him that
opportunity.

When we pray for ourselves, our petitions usually center
around what we think we need or what we are sure so-
and-so needs. God sees needs in our lives that are far more
urgent than those we have written on our heavenly super-
market list and daily present to our "Need-Meeter" in the
sky. Our need for changed attitudes, a new acceptance of
someone we have been rejecting, our need to be "cut down
to size"—these are not things we pray for too readily. On
the other hand, we do find we can pray these things for
other people!

Do you, for example, find yourself asking God to thoroughly humble you, or to give you the grand opportunity
to spend a lot of time with the very person you hate? Do
you hear yourself asking God to allow you to make an
absolute fool of yourself for Christ's sake?

When God told Jonah to go to Nineveh, it was not unre-
lated to Jonah's passionate request for his beleaguered

country. It was to be the beginning of the answer to his prayer. But, oh, the "much more" of God. He intended not only to meet Nineveh's and Israel's needs, but Jonah's need as well. *And,* incidentally, God's need would be met as He saw the results of the travail of His soul and would be satisfied. God was committed to making Jonah like His Son. God wanted him to learn to love what he had every right to hate, and to know the blessings that come to those who love their enemies.

I remember the day I realized God was committed to straightening me out. "The crooked *shall* be made straight" (Luke 3:5). The Bible says there are no crooked Christians allowed in God's camp! He is committed to making a highway for Himself through my life, and that means leveling the hills of pride and prejudice.

Even when I am not committed to "letting" Him straighten my crooked parts, my stubbornness, and my dislike of others who are not as I am, He is still committed to doing it. He overtakes me in my headlong plunge away from those "straightening" circumstances . . . just as He did with Jonah.

Jonah found it was useless to try to run away from God's instructions, because God has longer legs! Jonah had a truly "in-depth" experience over the whole thing!

Read Jonah 1 around the group or to yourself. Answer and discuss the following questions:
1. How did the heathen soldiers react to the great danger (vv. 5-7,13)?
2. What was God's gracious action toward them (v. 16)?

In the face of God's goodness to these ignorant men,

Hush! Hush!

Jonah's pigheadedness shows up all the more. Great may be my stubbornness, but greater always His faithfulness. I have found in my own spiritual experience that if I am struggling to accept His obvious way for me, resenting it all the time, then to see Him bless others around me (not nearly so deserving of blessing as myself!) results in more misery. Their blessing adds fuel to the flames of my unhappiness, and yet I am the *cause* of my own hurt! I run away while they run toward the God I fear. Like Jonah in 1:9, I fear but I flee. But not for long, for here comes the whale!

Read Jonah 2, then discuss the following questions, or work on your own.

1. Why did Jonah start praying again (vv. 2,7)?
2. How can we make sure this does not become a pattern of our prayer life?
3. What immediate assurances did Jonah receive (v. 2)?
4. How did the rebellious prophet bring himself back into touch with God (v. 4)? Were his mind, emotions, or will involved?
5. Affliction sharpens all our remembrances. Just what did Jonah remember (v. 9)?
6. God assures us of His control over the events of our lives (v. 10). Also see Romans 8:28,35-39 and Psalm 23.

   Spend a few minutes praying about what you have learned. What vows have you forgotten? Can you even begin to praise God for the whale?
7. If working in a group, one or two of you may share an experience you have had of rebellion against God's revealed will. Tell the group about the "whale" God used to bring you back!

Jonah 3:1 says, "And the word of the LORD came unto Jonah the second time"! Oh, the grace and mercy of God! But, notice *carefully* what "the word" was. "Go to Nineveh." The word was the same. Much had happened to Jonah to change his mind; nothing had changed in the mind of God. God's desire to spare heathen nations from judgment through personal and national repentance never changes, as Jeremiah 18:7-10 tells us. God's purposes remain the same. God's attitude toward a pouting prophet never varies either. He wanted to help Jonah understand that disobedience is sin! You see, until you obey the *last* command God gave you, He has nothing more to say. No new revelation, truth, or experience will be yours until you *do* the will of God concerning you. No new exciting concert piece until you have mastered the last one!

Now, I'm sure Jonah was desperate to hear the voice of God again. That was progress of a sort. I don't know quite what he expected to hear. Maybe, "Poor Jonah, I'm sorry I allowed that nightmarish thing to happen to you. I promise you I won't do it again." Maybe something like that? Well, all he heard was "Go to Nineveh," and he got mad. Mad but wiser, he decided he wasn't going to risk another whale. And so he simply set off getting madder and madder all the time!

Read chapters 3 and 4 in pairs or silently. Do you know what Jonah felt like? I do. Discuss.

When I first came to the United States, I asked God to use me with teen-agers. "Give me the hearts of the teen-agers of our church, Lord," I remember praying fervently. Instead He said, "Go to Nineveh." Nineveh in this instance

133

happened to be "women." I did not want to work with women. True, I am a woman, but I did not like to be among lots of women. God sent a "whale" to carry me to the place of His commandment. The "whale" was circumstance and duty. I was a pastor's wife and therefore could not escape groups of women. I was the wife of a prominent preacher and therefore *must* be able to speak as well as he (so the illogical reasoning usually goes).

Therefore, invitations began to come to me from all over the United States to address large gatherings of women. The "whale" took me there, and I preached as Jonah preached. I went grudgingly, stayed as short a time as possible, touched no one, nor allowed them to touch me, and marched out the other side of my assignment, to sit brooding about it all on my "hill of disdain." It touched me as little as it had touched Jonah that the people had received my message and responded. In fact, that made me as angry as Jonah, because it simply meant more unwelcome invitations!

Now if the Book of Jonah teaches me anything, it is this: Prayer can change my attitude concerning the will of God for my life. Prayer can change my feelings about Nineveh. And prayer can make a difference as to how I do the will of God. The biggest miracle of the Book of Jonah is his changed attitude. Remember, "great may be my stubbornness, but greater still Thy faithfulness about my stubbornness."

Read and discuss chapter 4 in pairs, or work on your own using a pencil and notebook. Answer the following questions:

1. *What does this chapter teach us about God (vv. 2,4,9-11)?*
2. *What does this chapter teach us about Jonah (vv.*

1,3,5,8)?
3. What does this chapter teach me about myself?
A question to ask and discuss after reading the Book of Jonah is, Was Jonah's attitude changed? Can we know? Think about it.

I believe Jonah's attitude *was* changed. Dr. Alan Redpath, in a series of lectures on the subject, pointed out that Jonah wrote the book! It is his testimony. It is an honest, open account of the arguments of the God who, in the debating chamber of the prophet's soul, won the debate! He is trying to tell us he came close to the heart of God concerning people. Even though the Assyrians were an unlovely, cruel people, Jonah discovered his anger and hatred were equally obnoxious to God, and he wanted to share his changed mind with us. "Doest thou well to be angry?" God had sternly inquired (4:4). Sin is sin. But people are people, and God loves! Should He not spare Nineveh? And should He not spare Jonah? Yes! Spared to spare others! Changed to change others! That is the testimony of this man of God, Jonah.

It is important to remember that God is just as concerned to see *how* we perform His will as He is that it gets performed. It is one thing to battle in prayer and become willing to be obedient, but it is another thing to do that will happily and hilariously—with glad anticipation and acceptance. Romans 12:2 states that the will of God is good and perfect and *acceptable*—not a bitter pill to swallow, but one with a sweet taste.

Listen to Jonah's "thought-talk" with God: "Lord, I don't like them, and they don't like me! I can't imagine why not when I'm so utterly desirable, but they think I'm a creep! Quite honestly, that is high praise compared to what I think of *them*. But don't worry; I'll deliver Your message and then make a quick getaway as usual. And help me to get an A again for my superb acting ability, because I know and You know I couldn't care two cents for them. But, Lord, *they* can't possible know *that,* can they?"

A bit far-fetched? I don't think so. And incidentally, the Ninevites *do* know you don't care. They know because even though your message is biblically correct, it is decorous and dead. Even though they acknowledge the truth of it, they feel nothing of the grace of it. How can they when you are a blocked, cold channel determined not to love?

Prayer is meant to be the key to open the dam, to release the waters of life, which is the love of God. And if you don't use the key and love them, *they will know it!*

Oh, how God has spoken to me in my prayer times and taught me to be *honest* with myself, with Him, and then with those against whom I have sinned. Prayer has revealed my poverty of spirit, my bigoted attitudes toward those I am sent to serve. In prayer God has shattered the ice of my soul and set me free to love! He has answered my prayers—not as I told Him to, praise God—but with a whale of a storm, a group of difficult people, or a seemingly impossible assignment. He has listened deeper than my superficial request and answered the hidden needs of my character. He has ignored my petitions for physical ease, and yet strangely answered them by giving me rest in distress, comfort in adversity, and joy in the midst of a Nineveh situation. Truly I can say, "I know not what I should pray for as I ought: but the Spirit itself maketh intercession for me with groanings that cannot be uttered!"

The secret is to spend time with God and draw close to Him. If you get close enough to hear God's heartbeat, then you'll get involved with people. Jonah allowed himself to get close enough to experience the throb of the heartbeat of the love of God for a lost nation (4:11). I like to think that when we get to eternity, Jonah will tell us about "his" people, those he lived with and loved along to maturity— the people of Nineveh. But, reader, how is it with *your* Jonah attitude? Don't run; keep praying. Don't dive over the side of your ship like Jonah did. God's whales are everywhere. You might as well stay and pray it out! But remember, it's dangerous when you begin to pray for other people. It always spells involvement.

You see, Jonah needed to learn to stop in the city—not outside it, but *in it*. And maybe that's what you and I have to learn too. Maybe you find yourself teaching a Sunday school class. You march into it at 9:30 A.M. on a Sunday morning, deliver your message, march out the other side at 10:30 A.M., and sit apart and reserved, criticizing your pupils until next Sunday morning. You are just like Jonah. You need to stop in the city and get involved in their lives!

Jesus was different. He left heaven, becoming the answer to His own prayer for us. He stopped in the city, and He totally identified with us, touching us, healing us, talking to us, living with us, and loving us. He then walked out the other side and back to heaven, but not before He had invited us all to come along!

The victory for me concerning my Nineveh of women was accomplished through prayer. I prayed as I went. True, my prayers were angry, resentful prayers like Jonah's; but I have learned that if my anger is to be turned into acceptance and my dislike into love, I must keep talking, and listening, and obeying. I also had to learn to stop in the city. I had to cease preaching *at* the women and begin to allow them to share themselves with me, to touch my life and heart. I had to be willing to feel their needs and empathize with their problems. I had to learn to identify.

Hush! Hush!

That takes time, effort, and trouble, but it's worth it. And it means that in time you may become the answer to your own prayer.

God didn't give me my heart's desire when I asked Him for the teen-agers. Or did He? He gave me their mothers, and *they* took the message to their children, which, after all, is as it is meant to be!

Don't resent the whale; let it take you to an understanding and appreciation of His will for you and His love and purposes for the very people for whom you are praying.

> *STOP NOW. Whether in a group or by yourself, tell God you're ready to start listening and receiving orders again. Don't be surprised to hear the same commands you heard at cut-off time years or months ago—just tell Him you will obey this time. And pray as you go to obey. Your prayers may be angry, but just keep talking. Don't shut off, and you'll see. God will win the debate, and you'll find yourself stopping in the city—a changed man, woman, or child. And God will get the glory!*

11

Why the Delay?

Where are You, Lord?

I have been so defeated by circumstances that I have felt like an animal trapped in a corner with nowhere to flee. Where are You in all this, Lord? The night is dark and I cannot feel Your presence.

Help me to know that the darkness is really the "shade of Your hand, outstretched caressingly"; that the "hemming in" is Your doing. Perhaps there is no other way I will allow You to demonstrate what You can do in my life. Therefore, in the strength of Christ's name, I pray. Amen.

11

Why the Delay?

The great enemy of our prayer life is Satan himself. It is he we battle when we attempt to pray. Prayer is the God-given atomic weapon against evil powers that Satan must prevent being used at all costs. Remember,

Satan trembles when he sees,
The weakest saint upon his knees.

1. *Read Ephesians 6:12 and make a list of the un-seen powers we wrestle against.*
2. *Read Ephesians 1:18-23 and answer these questions:*
   a. *Where is Christ now (v. 20)?*
   b. *What is His position above (v. 21)?*
   c. *What is His relationship to the church (v. 22)?*
   d. *Am I a part of His body (v. 23; 1 Cor. 12:12-14)?*

> e. What is my position in Christ in relation to the authorities and unseen wicked powers (v. 22; Eph. 1:3)?

The source of my authority is God who worked with a mighty power (Eph. 1:19). If I doubt how powerful He is, I can simply think of the demonstration of that power when God raised Christ from the dead! Someone has said, "The devil laughed at the cross, but stopped laughing at the Resurrection." In Him I can challenge the evil authority that holds fast the people who are without Christ, without hope, and without God on this earth.

> Christ has overcome Satan. Look up and discuss the following verses:
>
> 1. Luke 22:31-32
> 2. Colossians 2:15
> 3. 1 Peter 3:22
> 4. Revelation 12:7-12
> 5. Revelation 20:10

Like a traffic director in the midst of a traffic jam, I am invested with the authority of the government. I represent it, even though in my small person I am so much "less" than the cars I direct. When I raise my hand, I can confront and stop the traffic.

This power that enables me to stand in front of Satan "in Christ" has much to do with the wrestling of prayer.

There is an unseen battle going on before I even get in on the act. We have almost no idea what is happening a hidden sense away. You remember Elisha prayed that God would open his servant's eyes to see the unseen forces surrounding and protecting them, and God did just that for the discouraged and frightened servant.

He would do that for us as well. There are good spirits constantly working on our behalf in the heavenly places, just as surely as there are evil forces working against us and against those for whom we are praying.

Satan desires to destroy the mission of God. The sphere of moral struggle is therefore taken to the unseen world. Let us collect and share the data from the following verses concerning good and bad angels.

1. *Good angels—God's messengers to man. (Matt. 13:41,49; 18:10; 22:30; 24:36; 25:31; 26:53; Mark 8:38; Luke 15:10; 16:22; 1 Cor. 4:9; Eph. 3:10; Col. 2:18; Heb. 1:14; 1 Peter 1:12; Rev. 22:8ff)*
2. *Superior angels—Who and what are they called? (Ps. 8:5; Isa. 6:1-6; Ezek. 10:20; Dan. 8:15ff.; 9:21; Rev. 3:14; 5:2)*
3. *Bad angels—Matthew 25:41 teaches us Satan also has his angels. Gather information as to Satan's names, and facts about his demons' activities. (Matt. 4:3; 12:24; 13:19-39; John 8:44; 2 Cor. 6:15; 1 Thess. 3:5; 1 Peter 5:8; 1 John 2:13-14; Rev. 12:3,9)*

We are given a beautiful example of the conflict between the good and evil spirits in the Book of Daniel.

Read Daniel 10:1-9 on your own or in pairs.

For three full weeks Daniel had been praying and fasting, experiencing a great spirit of heaviness. He received a vision of God (vv. 5-6) which led to a sense of his own unworthiness. We have already talked about the effect a vision of God has on a man in our first study, and here we see a similar effect on Daniel (vv. 8-9). Another angel appears and touches Daniel, strengthening him and commanding him to stand upright. He reminds him how greatly God loves him and reassures him that the Father has seen his right attitude of heart, heard his prayer, and has immediately dispatched His angel emissary with the answer (v. 12). Then why three weeks' delay?

The most fantastic piece of information is given to Daniel in the following verses:

> But the prince of the kingdom of Persia withstood me one and twenty days: but, lo, Michael, one of the chief princes, came to help me; and I remained there with the kings of Persia. Now I am come to make thee understand what shall befall thy people in the latter days: for yet the vision is for many days. And when he had spoken such words unto me, I set my face toward the ground, and I became dumb. And, behold, one like the similitude of the sons of men touched my lips; then I opened my mouth, and spoke, and said unto him who stood before me, O my lord, by the vision my sorrows are turned upon me, and I have retained no strength. For how can the servant of this my lord talk with this my lord? for as for me, straightway there remained no strength in me, neither is there breath left in me. Then there came again and touched me one like the appearance of a man, he strengthened me, And said, O man greatly beloved, fear not: peace be unto thee, be strong, yea, be strong. And when he had spoken unto me, I was strengthened, and said, Let my lord speak; for thou hast strengthened me. Then said he, Knowest thou why I come unto thee? and now will I return to fight with the prince of Persia: and when I am gone forth, lo, the prince of Greece shall come. But I will show thee that which is noted in the scripture of truth; and there is none that holdeth with me in these things, but Michael, your prince. Also I in the first year of Darius the Mede, even I, stood to confirm and to strengthen him (Dan. 10:13–11:1).

144

Why the Delay?

The angel calmly explains to Daniel the reason for the delayed answer to his prayer. There may be many reasons for a "wait" answer from God, but one of the most stupendous ones is here in this chapter. There has been a spiritual battle going on. Evil angels have been withstanding good ones, who were sent to minister to Daniel.

So it is today—behind the mighty rulers of our world stand evil or good angels influencing them.

Not only do we have to contend with direct attacks of the evil one against us, but we must be aware that we enter a spiritual battlefield whenever we simply drop to our knees and say, "Our Father. . . ."

Like Moses, we have to learn that the "I Am" has sent us to stand before Pharaoh and demand with all of heaven's authority behind us that he let the people go! Satan, who stood behind that earthly Pharaoh, might tighten his grip upon the people as soon as we begin to pray, but if we rebuke him in the name of the Lord, because of our position in Christ, he will have no alternative but to give them up. It is then up to the people in bondage to exercise their free will and leave! The choice is theirs. God will not, and we must not, violate their right to choose. But praying "back" the forces of evil, while that choice is made, is a wrestling pastime that is the believer's privilege, yea, even his responsibility . . . that the air might be cleared around those we pray for so that God's voice may be clearly heard!

Hush! Hush!

*Exercise**

Each day this week, do the following:

1. In *prayer* take your seat with Christ (Eph. 1:3).
2. In *faith* take the name of Jesus as your Authority, believing the spiritual forces will yield.
3. *Watch* for humility as needed . . . as you see prayer working! Armor is needed in this spiritual battle. Read Ephesians 6:13-18. Make a list of God's gifts of protection for you.
4. *Rebuke the enemy!* We cry, "Rebuke Satan, Father!" He replies, *"My child, rebuke him yourself—*the Authority over him is yours!" Everything that is over your head is already under His feet and potentially under yours, too.
5. Have a *prayer time.* From the safety of your position in Christ, demand that Satan let go of certain people you know are in his grip. Remember that God is the Power over all evil powers. Learn 1 Peter 3:22 by heart!

*I would like to recommend the booklet *The Authority of the Believer* by Rev. J. A. MacMillan (Harrisburg, Penn.: Christian Publications, Inc., n.d.), from which I derived much help for this study.

146

12

Prayers of the Bible

Dearest Father,

Through Your Son, I come—shameful of the fact that I've neglected You; fearful of Your righteousness; trembling before Your holiness; humbled by Your everythingness; disgusted with the way I think I can hide things from You. It's tragic how I think I can handle my life on my own, when I panic if my car won't start. I guess I'm overwhelmed to think You've provided a way for insignificant little me to be with You forever. I pray that You will help me admit in my inner being, that I —all of me—am rightfully Yours to do with as You will. Praise You, Lord and Master. Amen.

Dear Father,

I thank You so much that You're always ready to teach me when my heart is willing and open, for I know it rarely is. Please forgive the doubts I have about You and Your Word. Thank You that You know what You're doing and that You don't make mistakes.

Sometimes it seems that You have a very special plan for my life—something special that You want me to do—yet I rebel, and my pride gets in the way. Please show me the same love and patience You showed Moses, because I, like Moses, need so much assurance. Make me willing to be used by You however You will. Thank You for loving me even when I forget You.

From my heart,
Sharon

12

Prayers of the Bible

One of the most helpful exercises in learning about prayer is to study the prayers of the Bible. There is no way in a book like this that I can give you full outlines for each prayer, but I will include a few ideas. You can work through the rest yourself.

Abraham's Prayers

Genesis 15:1-21. Study this chapter and make a list of the things God shared with Abraham. What did Abraham ask of God? Do these prayers appear to be selfish (vv. 2,8)?

Genesis 17:1-22. Study this passage and discuss Abraham's petition in verse 18. What did he learn of God as He answered him? What can we learn from this?

Genesis 18:23-33. We have already thought about this passage in the chapter entitled "Praying for Our Loved Ones." Write a summary of what you have learned.

Hush! Hush!

Genesis 20:17-18. Note the power of this man's prayers even when he had done the wrong thing!

Genesis 22:1-19. Read this through. The quiet time was a little one-sided here. God was doing all the speaking. What was the one thing Abraham said to God in this prayer time, and what can we learn from this?

Abraham's Servant's Prayer

Genesis 24:1-52. Good prayer habits rub off on those who observe them. Study Abraham's servant's prayer. Discuss the element of faith in verses 13-14, the way he tested the answer (v. 21), and his worship (v. 52). Discuss the ways we can ask God to show us specific "signs" and also the dangers of such requests. What do you think are some guidelines? In this respect, study Gideon's famous "fleece prayer" in Judges 6:37.

Jacob's Prayer

Genesis 32:24-30. Study this extraordinary incident and write down how we could apply it to the wrestling of God and man in prayer.

The Slave's Prayer

Exodus 2:23-25; 3:9-11. What do we learn of God's concern in relation to this sort of praying? What problems does God face in answering such prayers (3:11)?

Hannah's Prayers

1 Samuel 1:10-18. Note the intensity of Hannah's prayers. What effect did her problem have on her? What characteristics of trust did she display (v. 18)? Study 1 Samuel 2:1-10 and remember that she had just given her son away! What aspects of praise do we learn from this passage?

Moses' Prayers

Section I

Exodus 3. Moses had spent forty years in the desert, a convicted murderer hiding from Pharaoh. He was eighty years old when God called him to begin the work for which he was miraculously prepared. "Delivered to be a deliverer," his prayer-conversation with God concerning his call is recorded for us here.

Fill in the answers, working in pairs or individually.

1. What is the prerequisite to talking with God (v. 4)?
2. In what sort of place can we engage in prayer with God (v. 5)?
3. What word is used to describe what happens to the "ordinary" ground on which we stand or kneel to meet God (v. 5)?
4. What does God do for Moses at the beginning of his prayer time (v. 6)?
5. How can God do this for us today?

In verse 10 God reveals certain things to Moses and then issues a command. What are these things God reveals? How can we know the mind of God today and His personal call to us? Can we expect a burning bush? Discuss.

Prayer can be a place for argument. Moses felt free to tell God what he felt about His Word. Answer the following questions, working in pairs again.

6. What was Moses' feeling (v. 11)?
7. What was God's answer (v. 12)?
8. What was Moses' next problem (v. 13)?
9. What was God's answer and what did it mean (v. 14)?
10. God spent verses 13-22 reassuring him. Read them quickly to yourself. Did it help (Exod. 4:1)?
11. God gives Moses two miraculous signs (vv. 4-6 and

6-10). What two miraculous signs do we have to tell others about?

12. What was Moses' next complaint (v. 10)?
13. What was God's answer (vv. 11-12)?
14. What was Moses' response to the answer (v. 13)?

If God had wanted someone else, He would have asked someone else! God has to get tough (vv. 14-17)! Write a sentence about the lesson God wants you to learn today. Share that lesson with your partner and then pray for each other about it.

Section II: *How to Pray About Problems*

Numbers 11. What was Moses' problem (v. 1). List the children of Israel's complaints in verses 4-10. God was displeased with the children of Israel. Verse 10 says Moses also was displeased. With whom was he displeased? Write in your own words, as if you were Moses, his complaint in verses 11-15. What practical help did God give Moses in verses 16-23? How will He give us practical help today? Share an experience like this with each other.

Read Numbers 12, then role-play the passage. One member of the group should play the part of Miriam—state her attitude and complaint. Another should play Aaron—state his point of view. Someone else take the role of God—state His point of view. Another, taking the part of Moses, should pray his prayer for Miriam. Why was Moses' prayer gracious in the extreme? What does this teach you about your prayer life?

In Numbers 14:11-20 read how to pray for pardon for people who don't want to be pardoned!

1. What did God tell Moses He would do to the children of Israel and why (vv. 11-12)?
2. What were Moses' concerns as he prayed (vv. 13-19)?

152

Why did God hear Moses' prayers? For Moses' sake (vv. 20-21)?

This is the reason God answers prayer, and let us never forget it! Prayer produces heart concern for the people we minister to. See how far Moses has come from Exodus 3!

Numbers 16:20-22, 44-48: Verse 48 teaches and under-lines a principle of prayer we believers may exercise on others' behalf. What is it?

Numbers 27:12-17. We are now approaching the end of Moses' life. Discuss Moses' last prayer. What personal qualities has his relationship with God produced?

Read *Deuteronomy 33:10-12* — Moses' epitaph. *Pray about it!*

One good exercise is to choose people who would like to take other prayers of Bible characters, such as Daniel or Abraham, and work out a specific prayer study like this one for their group.

Samuel's Prayer

1 Samuel 3:1-18. Study Samuel's first prayer time with the living God! It was quite an experience. What method did God use to get his attention (v. 8)? What was the result of his first prayer time (vv. 15,18)? Note the ongoing re-sults (vv. 19-20). Discuss from this story the points we can note about teaching our children to pray, e.g., have them in God's house at all costs.

David's Prayers

Psalms. There are many passages we could look at, but I believe the main study should be Psalm 51, David's prayer of repentance. Take this psalm verse by verse and work your way through it, finding all the things you can learn about how to repent in prayer.

1 Chronicles 29:10-18. Another of David's special

"praise" prayers can be searched for rich language to adapt and use ourselves in thanksgiving.

Nehemiah's Prayers

Nehemiah 4:4-9. Verse 9 brings together prayer and the practical. Discuss whether the "watch" was a lack of faith or if we can learn something from this. If so, what?

Job's Prayer

Job 38–42. Take 15 minutes for the class to read this passage. When everyone has finished, have each share one thing God has reminded Job of concerning Himself.

Read 42:1-6. Have each person rewrite Job's prayer in modern English.

Did God give Job an answer to the "why" of suffering or simply reveal Himself as the Answer?

Isaiah's Prayer

Isaiah 6:1-8. We have already studied this passage in chapter 2. Go over the study with the group. Then read Isaiah's testimony concerning prayer in 40:31. Discuss and pray about this together.

Jonah's Prayer

The whole Book of Jonah can be taken chapter by chapter and studies on the different aspects of prayer discussed. Since it is an account of a man's prayer struggle concerning doing the will of God, it is richly rewarding. (Also see chapter 10.)

Jeremiah's Prayer

Jeremiah 1:4-10. This is a good prayer to study regarding witnessing. What were the man's problems and how did God reassure him?

Jeremiah 7:16. Discuss this dreadful statement. Read the context verses. What does it mean?

Jeremiah 10:19ff. List Jeremiah's "woes" in prayer. What are his requests for himself at this time?

Jeremiah 12:1-4. Jeremiah asks why. Does he get an answer (vv. 5-17)?

Jeremiah 15:15-21. Jeremiah prays about his persecutors. What does he pray and what is God's answer? Also read Jeremiah 20:7-18.

Jesus Debates Satan

Matthew 4:1-11. Study and learn all you can about Satan's wiles regarding prayer from this passage. Make notes on how Jesus dealt with him.

The Pharisee and the Publican

Luke 18:9-14. Make lists of do's and don'ts of prayer that this parable teaches us.

First-Century Christians' Prayer

Acts 4:23-31. Discuss the way the first-century Christians encouraged each other under persecution.

Ananias's Prayer

Acts 9:10-17. Discuss Ananias' prayer experience and his obedience to the difficult command. Apply the lessons learned.

Paul's Prayers

Section I

Philippians 1:3-11. Read the passage and then answer the following questions.

1. What spirit characterized Paul's prayer life (vv. 3-4)?

2. List Paul's reasons for praise on their behalf (vv. 5-6).
3. Describe Paul's feelings for these people (vv. 7-8).
4. List some of Paul's joyful requests (vv. 9-11).
5. The fruits he prays will be evident in their lives are listed in Galatians 5:22-23. List them.

Place someone's name beside the particular fruit of the Spirit you know the Lord would like to see manifest in his or her life. Then pray in pairs for these people.

Section II

Ephesians 1:15-23. Read the passage and then answer the following questions.
1. What stimulates Paul to pray (v. 15)?
2. With what spirit does he begin (v. 16)?
   a. Share examples of people who are full of faith and love.
   b. Thank God in prayer for them.
3. What does Paul pray for these people (v. 17)?
   a. Do you know anyone who needs that? Write down name.
   b. Verse 18: Who needs their eyes opened to all this? Write down name.
   c. Verse 19: Do you know anyone who needs power? Write down name.
4. Pray in pairs for these things for these people.
5. Read verses 20-23.
   a. What is our position in Christ?
   b. Where has He placed all things?

That means all that is over my head is under His feet! And, therefore, under *my* feet! *Remember,* the *victory* is yours in *Him!*

Take the following prayers of Paul and pray them for another. For example, using *Ephesians 1:16-23, begin like* this:

> Cease not to give thanks for *Ann*, making mention of her in my prayers; That the God of our Lord Jesus Christ, the Father of glory, may give unto *Ann* the spirit of wisdom and revelation in the knowledge of him: The eyes of *Ann's* understanding being enlightened; that *she* may know what is the hope of his calling, and what the riches of the glory of his inheritance in the saints, and what is the exceeding greatness of his power toward *Ann* who believes, according to the working of his mighty power, which he wrought in Christ, when he raised him from the dead, and set him at his own right hand in the heavenly places, far above all principality, and power, and might, and dominion, and every name that is named, not only in this age, but also in that which is to come; and hath put all things under his feet, and gave him to be the head over all things to the church, which is his body, the fullness of him that filleth all in all.

If you are working in pairs, this can be a very moving experience: taking turns, pray the great apostle's able and rich words for each other. Other suggested prayers are found in Ephesians 1:16-23; Philippians 1:9-11; and Colossians 1:9-13.

Epilogue

A mother was preparing for dinner guests one evening, so she reminded her little girl to say her prayers before she went to bed.

Next morning, the mother asked, "Did you say your prayers last night?"

"Well," the little one explained, "I got down on my knees and started to say them, and all of a sudden I thought: I bet God gets awfully tired hearing the same old prayer over and over.

"So I crawled into bed and told Him the story of the three bears."

I don't intend you to start telling God fairy stories, but I agree with the little girl! God must get pretty tired hearing the same old prayers over and over again from some of us. Maybe now we will begin to "say something" relevant and real to our heavenly Father.

In the front of my Bible I have a prayer. It is a little sentence I look at every time I rise to speak to an audience. It says: "O Lord, deliver me from the art of 'almost' saying something." I trust He has delivered me from doing just that in this book, and I pray that from this point on He will save us all from "almost" saying something to Him.

JILL BRISCOE

For Further Study

Allen, Charles L. *Prayer Changes Things*. Old Tappan, N.J.: Spire Books, 1973.

Bisagno, John. *Power of Positive Praying*. Grand Rapids: Zondervan, 1965.

Blaiklock, E. M. *The Positive Power of Prayer*. Glendale, Calif.: Regal, 1974.

Chadwick, S. *God Listens*. Westchester, Ill.: Good News Pub.

Christenson, Evelyn and Viola Blake. *What Happens When Women Pray*. Wheaton, Ill.: Victor Press, 1975.

Fife, Eric. *Prayer, Common Sense and the Bible*. Grand Rapids: Zondervan, 1976.

Goforth, Rosalind. *How I Know God Answers Prayer*. Chicago: Moody.

Gutzke, Manford G. *Plain Talk on Prayer*. Grand Rapids: Baker, 1973.

Haden, Ben. *Pray!* New York: Thomas Nelson Pub., 1974.

Hallesby, O. *Prayer*. Minneapolis: Augsburg, 1975.

Hanne, John A. *Prayer or Pretense?* Grand Rapids: Zondervan, 1974.

MacDonald, Hope. *Discovering How to Pray*. Grand Rapids: Zondervan, 1976.

Miller, Basil. *George Mueller: Man of Faith*. Minneapolis: Bethany Fellowship, 1972.

Rhea, Carolyn. *Come Pray With Me*. Grand Rapids: Zondervan, 1977.

Rinker, Rosalind. *Prayer—Conversing With God*. Grand Rapids: Zondervan, 1959.

————. *Praying Together*. Grand Rapids: Zondervan, 1968.

Stedman, Ray C. *Jesus Teaches on Prayer*. Waco, Tex.: Word, 1975.

Strauss, Lehman. *Sense and Nonsense About Prayer*. Chicago: Moody, 1974.

Torrey, R. A. *How to Pray*. Old Tappan, N.J.: Spire Books, 1970.

———. *The Power of Prayer*. Grand Rapids: Zondervan, 1971.

Townsend, Anne J. *Prayer Without Pretending*. Chicago: Moody, 1976.

Unknown Christian. *The Kneeling Christian*. Grand Rapids: Zondervan, 1971.

Wallis, Arthur. *God's Chosen Fast*. Fort Washington, Pa.. Christian Literature Crusade, 1970.